SUPER HEROES

Studies in Popular Culture
M. Thomas Inge, General Editor

SUPER HEROES

A Modern Mythology

Richard Reynolds

University Press of Mississippi
Jackson

First published by B. T. Batsford Ltd., London
First published in 1994 in the United States of America
by the University Press of Mississippi
Manufactured in the United States of America

97 96 95 94 4 3 2 1

The paper in this book meets the guidelines for permanence and durability of the Committee on Production Guidelines for Book Longevity of the Council on Library Resources.

Library of Congress Cataloging-in-Publication Data

Reynolds, Richard.
Super heroes : a modern mythology / Richard Reynolds.
p. cm. — (Studies in popular culture)
Originally published: London : B.T. Batsford, c1992. (Batsford cultural studies)
Includes bibliographical references and index.
ISBN 0-87805-693-9 (cloth). — ISBN 0-87805-694-7 (paper)
1. Comic books, strips, etc.—United States—History and criticism.
2. Heroes—United States. I. Title. II. Series: Studies in popular culture (Jackson, Miss.)
[PN6725.R48 1994]
741.5'0973—dc20 93-48411
CIP

CONTENTS

ACKNOWLEDGEMENTS

The Author and Publisher would like to thank DC Comics for their permission to reproduce material featuring their trademarked characters on pages 11, 13, 21, 31, 33, 39, 42, 64, 71, 72, 78, 99, 104, 112 and on the front cover. Acknowledgement is also made to Marvel Comics for the use of material featuring their trademarked characters on pages 28, 35, 36, 55, 56, 59, 76, 87, 90 and 93. The Avengers, Captain America, Iron Man, the She-Hulk, Thor, the X-Men and the distinctive likenesses thereof are trademarks of the Marvel Entertainment Group, Inc. © 1994 and are used with permission. Thanks are also due to the Victoria and Albert Museum and to David Pratt for their help with photography.

The author would also like to thank John Izod for his help and encouragement at all stages of this book's development, as well as Steve Edgell, Lindsay Porter and Ian Rakoff for their criticisms and comments on the final draft.

1 Masked Heroes

Batman, Superman, Spider-Man, Wonder Woman; among the most widely-known fictional characters ever conceived. Created as comic-book heroes, they remain more widely known through television, the movies and (in the case of Batman and Superman) through a vigorous presence in American and European popular culture that ensures their recognition by millions who have never read a Batman comic or seen a Superman film. Superman, Batman and Wonder Woman[1] have remained continuously in print and involved in an unbroken sequence of new adventures for over 50 years. Yet the medium from which they spring – the 6×9in 4-colour comic book – continues to be (at least in American and British culture) a marginalized channel of communication held by many to be an irredeemably corrupt and corrupting form of discourse, or else suitable only for children and the semi-literate.

In consequence, the adult superhero readership (a sub-section of the adult comic readership as a whole) has come to identify itself as a small and very cohesive subculture. Specialist comic-book retailers, 'marts' and full-scale conventions are the outward signs of this cohesion, as is the highly-organized market-place for buying, selling and collecting old comics. If connoisseurship and value to the collector alone gave access to the privileged world of high culture, superhero comics would have been there long ago.

For the cultural student, superhero comics present a number of immediate paradoxes: a popular art-form traditionally known for its apparently hegemonic and sometimes overtly authoritarian texts; a publishing genre which began to gain a degree of cultural respectability by ducking 'underground' at least partially for its distribution; an art-form which has been handled (if at all) with disdain by the literary establishment, and yet has built up its own lively and heuristic critical discourse through what is still rather misleadingly known as the 'fan' press;[2] and, finally, a body of contemporary mythology from which television and Hollywood have plundered material as diverse as the campy 1960s Batman TV show, the apparent artlessness of the Christopher Reeve Superman cycle, and the overwrought gothic bravura of the 1989 Batman movie.

The superhero genre is tightly defined and defended by its committed readership – often to the exasperation of writers and artists, many of whom have proclaimed it to be a worn-out formula from as long ago as the 1970s. But the dinosaur refuses to keel over and die, and dominates the economics of the American comics industry. The chief superhero characters remain its most widely-understood and recognized creations – to the annoyance of writers and artists who would like to bring the wider possibilities of the comic book (or graphic novel)[3] to the attention of the general public.

An attempt to define the limits of the genre can best be made as part of a broader exploration of the heroes themselves – differing as they do from each other sometimes as much as Gandhi and the Lone Ranger. The costumed superhero burst into seemingly fully-fledged existence in June 1938, with the appearance on American newsstands of *Action Comics* 1, featuring Superman's first ever appearance in print. The new arrival proved enormously popular, and quickly led to a host of imitations and new ideas along similar lines – from Batman, Wonder Woman, and the Sub Mariner – all with us to this day – to such obscure creations as The Arrow, Shock Gibson and the Masked Marvel.[4]

America's entry into World War Two gave the superheroes a whole new set of enemies, and supplied a complete working rationale and world view for a super-patriotic superhero such as Captain America.[5] This so-called Golden Age[6] of comics and superhero comics in particular lasted up to the late 1940s, when the bulk of the costumed superhero titles folded as a result of falling readerships. Only Superman, Batman and Wonder Woman came through the lean years of the early 1950s without a break in publication. The spotlight had shifted elsewhere – to crime comics, western comics, horror comics.

As is well known, it was the excesses of the horror comics which led indirectly to the renaissance of the superhero genre. The bloody guts and gore of Entertaining Comics'[7] *Tales From the Crypt*, *Vault of Horror*[8] and other titles both from EC and rival publishers led to the censorious publication *Seduction of the Innocent*[9] by Dr Frederic Wertham and the 1954 Congressional hearings on juvenile delinquency and comics.[10] The comic publishers responded to the adverse publicity of the report and the hearings with the self-censoring Comics Code – still extant today. The Code involved a voluntary ban by the publishers themselves on violence, explicit sex, gratuitous gore and the triumph of evil or antisocial behaviour. In a move against the 'true crime' comics which had peaked in popularity in the late 1940s, the Code stipulated that law enforcement officers should never be shown in a disrespectful or unsympathetic light.

Clearly, the climate had changed. Detective Comics (DC) decided to expand their small list of superhero comics which had, in the early 1950s, shrunk to no more than Superman, Batman and

Wonder Woman. A re-born and re-costumed Flash (1956)[11] paved the way for the return of the Green Lantern (1959),[12] a new heroine, Supergirl (1959)[13] and then a whole superhero team in the shape of the Justice League of America (1960).[14] Under the editorship of Stan Lee, Marvel Comics re-entered the superhero market with new titles such as *The Fantastic Four* (1961),[15] *Spider-Man*[16] (1963) and the *X-Men* (1964).[17] Norse Gods were added to the genre with *The Mighty Thor*,[18] and horror wedded to the superhero format in *The Incredible Hulk*.[19] Golden Age characters such as Captain America and the Sub Mariner were brought back out of retirement.[20]

This is the period usually referred to as the Silver Age, dating from the revival of the Flash in 1956. Marvel dominated the scene in the 1960s and early 1970s, its writers and artists creating a wealth of exciting new titles that mixed protagonists more in tune with the mores of the period, and kept an eye for the visual and verbal ironies inherent in situating super-powered characters against a background that purported to represent the 'real' world. It was the Marvel line of this period which first began the expansion of comics into a teenage and college readership. DC, however, remained the leading publisher of superhero comics in terms of sales, benefitting from the enormous appeal of the 1960s' Batman TV series. Batman and Superman titles made up nine of the ten best-selling comics in the USA by 1969. DC also developed innovative titles of its own, such as the Green Lantern/Green Arrow team-up of the early 1970s, which featured artwork by exciting new talent Neal Adams.[21]

But by the 1980s, the Marvel phenomenon had gone stale. DC reasserted itself as the leading comic book publisher, by means of a shrewd and imaginative revamping of its classic titles, and the promoting of exciting and innovative work both in the superhero genre (such as *Watchmen*), and in the linked genres of fantasy and horror, with titles such as *Hellblazer*. By the mid-1980s the Comics Code, once a force powerful enough to bring even EC's William Gaines to heel, had become a spent force, with both Marvel and DC insouciantly advertising many of their comics as 'Suggested for Mature Readers'. Such confidence in the labelling bespoke the strength of their adult readership. There is currently a feeling amongst some comic publishers that the 'adult' trend may have gone too far, and that comics may be running the risk of provoking another Wertham-like backlash against explicit violence and sexuality.[22]

Superman, the first superhero, was conceived by the teenage Jerry Siegel as early as 1934, lying sleepless one night in bed:

> I am lying in bed counting sheep when all of a sudden it hits me. I conceive a character like Samson, Hercules, and all the strong men I have ever heard tell of rolled into one. Only more so. I hop right out of

> bed and write this down, and then I go back and think some more for about two hours and get up again and write that down. This goes on all night at two hour intervals, until in the morning I have a complete script.[23]

But the concept of a character with superhuman strength and invulnerability was simply too unfamiliar for the comic book publishers of the early 1930s. Siegel and artist Joe Shuster established themselves in the comics business with the private eye strip 'Slam Bradley' (1934). Superman finally made his debut in *Action Comics* 1 (1938),[24] using material hastily adapted by Siegel and Shuster from a story which had originally been intended to form part of a newspaper strip.

Superman's arrival created a wholly new genre out of a very diverse set of materials. Today, many aspects of the first Superman story and its narrative approach have the appearance of cliché: it is necessary to keep in mind that the origin of what later became clichés lies right here.

Page 1 introduces the reader to the dying planet Krypton (unnamed), and explains that 'a scientist' has placed his infant son in a spaceship, launching it towards earth. The 'sleeping babe' is discovered and grows up in an orphanage (Clark Kent's parents in Smallville are a later addition to the mythology). On reaching maturity, the young man discovers that he can

> leap ⅛ mile, hurdle a twenty story building . . . raise tremendous weights . . . run faster than an express train . . .[25]

Moreover 'nothing less than a bursting shell' can penetrate his skin. Considerable powers, though modest when compared with the god-like abilities Superman would acquire later in his career. Clark decides to dedicate his strength to the benefit of mankind, and elects to assume the identity of Superman – all this in the first page of the story, which concludes with a 'scientific' explanation of Clark's superhuman abilities, comparing his strength with the proportionate strength of ants and grasshoppers. Pure hokum, but anticipating by 25 years Stan Lee's Spider-Man, and that character's 'proportionate strength of a spider'.

Pages 2–4 relate how Superman prevents an innocent woman going to the electric chair. On page 5 reporter Clark gets an assignment from the (unnamed) editor of the paper which employs him, the *Daily Star* (later to be renamed the *Daily Planet*):

> Did you ever hear of Superman?
>
> What?
>
> Reports have been streaming in that a fellow with gigantic strength

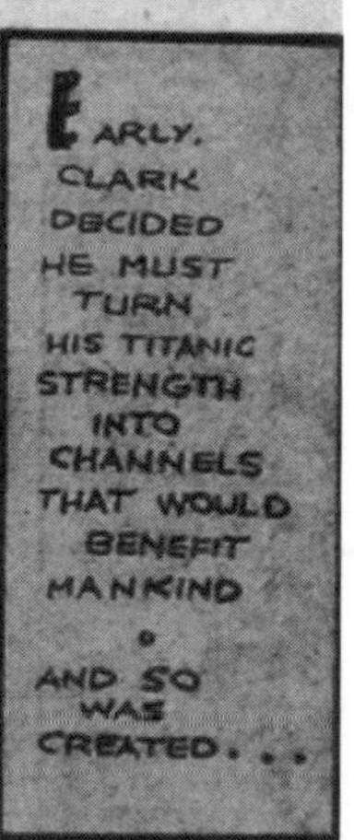

***Action Comics* 1, page 1. A complex mix of narrative and exposition, adapted from material produced for a newspaper strip.**

> named Superman actually exists. I'm making it your steady assignment to cover these reports. Think you can handle it, Kent?
>
> Listen Chief, if I can't find out anything about this Superman, no one can![26]

Pages 5–6 see Superman intervene in a wife-beating ('You're not fighting a woman now!'). Next, Clark encounters his smart and stylish colleague Lois Lane ('What do you say to a . . . er . . . date tonight, Lois?' 'I suppose I'll give you a break . . . for a change'). At the roadhouse, however, Clark is hustled away from his date by brawling Butch Matson, who has nothing but contempt for Clark's pacifist attitudes ('Fight . . . you weak livered polecat!' 'Really, I have no desire to do so!').

Lois leaves the club in disgust, but finds herself bundled into Matson's car. But even as they hustle their captive away, Matson and his cronies find the road blocked by the imposing figure of Superman, who tips both Lois and the roughnecks out of the car and then trashes the automobile, in a panel which also provides the subject matter for the comic's famous car-throwing cover. Superman carries Lois to safety, and on page 10 we find her telling the *Daily Star*'s editor of her meeting with the Man of Steel. Clark in the meantime has been given an assignment to visit the South American republic of San Monte to stir up news for the *Star's* front page. Instead, he travels to Washington DC to investigate a case of corruption in the US Senate ('The bill will be passed before its full implications are realized. Before any remedial steps can be taken, our country will be embroiled with Europe'). A cliff-hanger has Superman and the captured foreign agent failing to complete a leap between two adjacent skyscrapers.

Much that would become central to the superhero genre is established in these 13 pages. As a first step towards a definition of the superhero, some of the features of the story could be listed as follows:

1. Lost parents

A key preoccupation, discussed at greater length in chapter three. Superman is separated from his natural parents, and so his extraordinary powers are not represented in a straightforward parent-to-child relationship. Few superheroes enjoy uncomplicated relationships with parents who are regularly present in the narrative.

2. The man-god

The language of the story's first page mimics the King James Bible. A 'passing motorist, discovering the sleeping babe within' echoes the

Problems already for Clark Kent as Superman steals Lois Lane's affections: *Action Comics* 1. This page is conceived as a single narrative and structural unit, unlike the illustration on p.11.

Magi on the road to Bethlehem, or Moses among the bullrushes – both clearly appropriate notes to strike. The sky-spanning spaceship crashes into the Earth, leaving – in later versions of the myth, at least – a deep gash in the soil. So Superman is born from a marriage of Uranus (Heaven) and Gaia (Earth). In due course, Superman will acquire his Father on Earth (Kent senior) to go with Jor-El of Krypton, his Father in Heaven.

3. Justice

Superman's devotion to 'those in need' involves coming to the help of those victimized by a blind though well-intentioned state. Superman's first ever exploit involves breaking into the State Governor's bedroom in order to save an innocent woman from the electric chair. Superman does, however, leave the real murderer bound and gagged on the Governor's lawn.[27]

4. The normal and the superpowered

The momentary (illusory) power of the individual who threatens the superhero with a gun, knife or speeding car leads with deliberate inevitability to the astonished realization of the superhero's invulnerability. This is a note that most superhero stories strike from time to time, lest the contrast between super-powered hero and the average individual becomes lost – and the sense of wonder blunted by showing nothing but superpowered characters slugging it out with each other.

Page 3 of *Action Comics* 1 includes a fine use of this contrast linked to the structure of the panels and the necessity of turning the page to follow the story. The final panel of page 3 shows the Governor's butler firing a revolver at Superman from point blank range. Page 4, panel 1, shows an unharmed Superman reaching out to grab the revolver.

5. The secret identity

Why doesn't Clark let Lois know that he's Superman? The discourse of the story, the soap-opera continuity which investigates the Clark/Lois/Superman triangle, would be shattered if Lois were to realize Clark and Superman's unity. The Clark/Superman duality needs a constant supply of new dramatic situations to reveal new facets of the hero's split personality. The explicit reasons given within the story – such as 'They could use my friends to get at me', reasons which have become common throughout the genre, and do not need to be spelt out when establishing a new character – are only secondary to the structural need for characters to have secret identities.

This first-ever Superman story establishes the convention by using it as if it already existed. The reader is called upon to adduce adequate reasons for the disguise. And Lois's extreme scorn for the 'morning-after' Clark establishes the width of the Clark/Superman gulf by way of a one-sided conversation:

> I'm sorry about last night –
> please don't be angry with me.[28]

But Lois coldly stares in the opposite direction. She has become a different person from the warm and yielding individual Superman held in his arms just two panels before: panels which occupy opposite ends of a three-panel sequence in the centre of the page. The visual distance between Superman and Lois in the left-hand panel is similar to the distance which separates them on the right, but the emotional relationships implied by the figures are wholly different.

What has been established is in the nature of a taboo. Refraining from a certain act (in this case, revealing oneself to be Superman) wards off a potential disaster. Illogical perhaps, but the situation strengthens the appeal of our hero by establishing certain specific restraints which are peculiar to him and him alone. He pays for his great powers by the observance of this taboo of secrecy – in a manner which is analagous to the process in which warriors in many traditional societies 'pay' for their strength in battle by abstaining from sex, eating special foods, and other taboos designed to isolate and protect the 'masculine' in their characters.[29] Such concern with what amount to the rites of passage from adolescence to manhood is clearly of interest and concern to a teenage audience.

6. Superpowers and politics

The theme of restraint and limitation leads rather nicely to the question of the superheroes and the politicians. In fact, this theme is only lightly touched on in *Action Comics* 1. All that is established is Superman's ability (and willingness) to act clandestinely and even illegally if he believes that national interests may be at stake. His loyalty and patriotism are above even his devotion to the law. This entails some important consequences for a superhero such as Superman, who is beyond the power of the armed forces, should he choose to oppose state power. Endless story possibilities can be designed around the theme of the superhero wrestling with his conscience over which order should be followed – moral or political, temporal or divine.

7. Science as magic
This feature is fundamental to the nature of the universe which the superhero comic portrays. Science is treated as a special form of magic, capable of both good and evil. Scientific concepts and terms are introduced freely into plots and used to create atmosphere and add background detail to artwork – but the science itself is at most only superficially plausible, often less so, and the prevailing mood is mystical rather than rational. Explicitly 'magic' powers are able to coexist quite comfortably with apparently scientific ones. A good example of this is the partnership between Iron Man (science) and Thor (magic) developed over the years in Marvel's *Avengers* title. This question is discussed more fully in chapter three.

Although further removed from the character of the heroes themselves than the other points raised above, the depiction of science as magic is crucial to the way in which the superhero comic mythologizes certain aspects of the society it addresses. This question is followed up in chapter three.

These seven headings can be pulled together to construct a first-stage working definition of the superhero genre; a definition which at least has the authenticity of being constructed from the motifs of the first ever superhero comic.

1. The hero is marked out from society. He often reaches maturity without having a relationship with his parents.
2. At least some of the superheroes will be like earthbound gods in their level of powers. Other superheroes of lesser powers will consort easily with these earthbound deities.
3. The hero's devotion to justice overrides even his devotion to the law.
4. The extraordinary nature of the superhero will be contrasted with the ordinariness of his surroundings.
5. Likewise, the extraordinary nature of the hero will be contrasted with the mundane nature of his alter-ego. Certain taboos will govern the actions of these alter-egos.
6. Although ultimately above the law, superheroes can be capable of considerable patriotism and moral loyalty to the state, though not necessarily to the letter of its laws.
7. The stories are mythical and use science and magic indiscriminately to create a sense of wonder.

Turning some of these laws on their heads, such as 3 and 6, would give us a good working definition of the superhero's opponent, the supervillain. Such characters are implicit in the set of governing codes supplied to Superman in his first ever appearance, although they did not become a regular feature of superhero comics until around 1940.[30]

The early Superman stories were a resounding success. Readers asked for more of 'That magazine with Superman in it.' Publisher Harry Donenfield – initially sceptical – realized that he had a phenomenal success on his hands. The superhero market boomed. By 1942, several dozen superhero titles were on the American market, forming the largest share of the 150-odd individual comic-book titles on sale. Some were blatant copies of Superman: a lawsuit killed Fox Features' Wonderman, and another case was soon outstanding against Fawcett's Captain Marvel.[31] Other characters only derived from the Superman model in the most generic way: famous heroes already well-established included Batman, The Human Torch, The Sub Mariner, Captain America, Hawkman, Wonder Woman and the Green Lantern.[32] The new medium had created a new genre all its own, and one perfectly suited for the comic-book's ability to create unfettered fantasy at a price that even children could afford. Moreover, the idealistic but law-abiding superheroes fitted the mood of a United States about to go to war against the fascist powers.

Budgetary considerations make the superhero particularly suitable for the comics medium. Parallels can be drawn between the comic book and the cinema, but in one respect the two media are totally unalike. Film is an expensive art form. Budgets for feature films today rarely go lower than $4 million – they may go as high as $50 million or more. Comics are cheaper, and they are cheaper just where the cinema is most expensive. It costs DC comics no more to have John Byrne draw Superman replacing a space-station in orbit or bathing on the surface of a star, than to show Clark Kent crossing the street on his way to the office. Clearly, any film producer has a much tougher and tightly constrained set of choices to make about a project which may be perfectly sound when viewed simply from the angle of character and plot development.

The comic artist develops a familiarity, indeed almost a casual ease, in handling extraordinary and exotic locations. Such scenes can be casually introduced, for a few panels only, or a bewildering variety of settings can be made use of in one story, if required. The film producer, having decided to let his director build one or two expensive sets, is more or less obliged to 'shoot the money' – i.e. to make all this costly set-building pay off as part of the climactic action of the movie. Often this presents no insoluable problems, but it remains an additional pressure on story structure from which the comic-book artist-writer team remain refreshingly free.

Superman and the superhero emerged at the end of the Great Depression and during the run-up to the outbreak of the European war. Millions of Americans had experienced poverty and unemployment, millions more had had their faith in the notion of uninterrupted economic progress seriously undermined. Avenging 'Lone Wolf' heroes abounded in popular narrative of the 1930s and '40s on both sides of the Atlantic: from Doc Savage to Philip Marlowe, from Hannay in Hitchcock's *39 Steps* to the Green Hornet, from Rick Blaine in *Casablanca* to Captain Midnight[33] of the radio serials. A new kind of popular hero had emerged: the self-reliant individualist who stands aloof from many of the humdrum concerns of society, yet is able to operate according to his own code of honour, to take on the world on his own terms, and win. For Americans, the historical path from Munich to Pearl Harbor coincides with the emergence of Superman and Captain America – solitary but socialized heroes, who engage in battle from time to time as proxies of US foreign policy. A darker side of the Lone Wolf hero is embodied by the Batman, a hero whose motivations and emotions are turned inward against the evils within society, and even the social and psychological roots of crime itself. The tension between these two veins in the superhero tradition remains to the present day.

The locus of superhero comics was then, as it largely remains, New York. Writers and artists living in the city depict it in their work – so successfully that superhero stories set in any other city may require a certain degree of justification for their choice of locale. The New York of the early 1940s was a place seemingly chosen for the preservation of the values of European civilization, and a destination for large numbers of artists and intellectuals seeking refuge from the Nazi conquest of Europe: Auden, Isherwood, Ernst, Tanguy, Mondrian. The anthropologist Claude Levi-Strauss described his reactions on arriving in the city in the essay 'New York in 1941'.

> The French surrealists and their friends settled in Greenwich Village, where, just a few subway stops from Times Square, one could still lodge – just as in Balzac's time – in a small two- or three-story house with a tiny garden in back. A few days after my arrival, when visiting Yves Tanguy, I discovered and immediately rented, on the street where he lived, a studio whose windows faced a neglected garden. You reached it by way of a long basement corridor leading to a private stairway in the rear of a red-brick house . . . Just two or three years ago, I learned that Claude Shannon had also lived there, but on an upper story and facing the street. Only a few yards apart, he was creating cybernetics and I was writing *Elementary Structures of Kinship*. Actually, we had a mutual friend in the house, a young woman,

> and I recall that, without mentioning his name, she once spoke to me about one of our neighbours, who, she explained, was busy 'inventing an artificial brain.'
>
> . . . If I did not have it now before my eyes, it would be hard to believe that I bought one day a sixteenth-century Tuscan sideboard for a few dollars. However, New York (and this is the source of its charm and its peculiar fascination) was then a city where anything seemed possible. Like the urban fabric, the social and cultural fabric was riddled with holes. All you had to do was pick one and slip through if, like Alice, you wanted to get to the other side of the looking glass and find worlds so enchanting that they seemed unreal.[34]

This is the New York (or Gotham City, or Metropolis) that dominates the superhero story and has become its almost inevitable milieu. New York draws together an impressive wealth of signs, all of which the comic-reader (of the 1940s or the 1990s) is adept at deciphering. It is a city which signifies all cities, and, more specifically, all modern cities, since the city itself is one of the signs of modernity. It is the place where – since the comedies of Terence – the author takes the reader in order that something may be made to happen. And New York has always been the great point of disembarkation in the history and mythology of the New World (although today, Ellis Island has been opened as a museum and migration now occurs through El Paso, Los Angeles or Miami). New York is a sign in fictional discourse for the imminence of such possibilities – simultaneously a forest of urban signs and an endlessly wiped slate on which unlimited designs can be inscribed – cop shows, thrillers, comedies, 'ethnic' movies such as *Mean Streets*, *Moonstruck* or *Do The Right Thing*, and cyclical adventures of costumed heroes as diverse as Bob Kane's *Batman* and Alan Moore's *Watchmen*.

Artists and characters might even rub shoulders with each other on Madison Avenue. Marvel under Stan Lee and Jim Shooter has often blurred the distinction between New York as fictional milieu and New York as publishing centre – as in Doctor Doom's appearance in the Marvel Offices in *Fantastic Four* 10, explaining his escape from a runaway meteor.[35]

Sometimes a thin disguise is the easiest way of summoning up an all-too-familiar subject. Batman writer Bill Finger describes the origin of a famous by-name in the following way:

> Originally, I was going to call Gotham City 'Civic City'. Then I tried Capital City, then Coast City. Then I flipped through the phone book and spotted the name Gotham Jewellers and said 'That's it, Gotham City'. We didn't call it New York because we wanted anybody in any city to identify with it. Of course, Gotham is another name for New York.[36]

New York, however, couldn't be done away with so easily. The 1940 story 'Batman and Robin visit the 1940 New York World's Fair'[37] is one of the earliest stories involving Robin, the Boy Wonder. The story commences with Bruce Wayne and his young ward Dick Grayson striding towards the Fair, taking in and being impressed by everything they see.

Dick: Wow! I heard it was big, but I didn't think it was this big!

Bruce: Big is a mild word! It's stupendous . . . Look over there! – the trylon and the perisphere!

Dick: Say, let's go inside the perisphere! . . . And see the city of tomorrow.[38]

Clearly, it's appropriate that Bruce and Dick should spend their time keeping themselves abreast of the latest developments in technology, the better to prosecute their joint war against crime. Where better to do this than at New York's World's fair? But the off-duty Caped Crusaders have barely begun their day of enjoyment when they are faced with an unwelcome interruption: a radio exhibit broadcasting the news that the great Westriver Bridge has just melted away 'as if someone had played an acetylene torch upon it.' Bruce and Dick leave the World's Fair to investigate – but without changing into their costumes.

Wayne visits Commissioner Gordon and quizzes him about the bridge. While he's in the Commissioner's office, a Mr Travers of Travers Engineering arrives carrying a blackmail note which threatens destruction of a second bridge unless a ransom of $300,000 is paid. Commissioner Gordon advises Travers to ignore the threat – 'Probably a crackpot trying to cash in on easy money.' Meanwhile, Dick inspects the site of the disaster. Two men attack a woman. Dick intervenes, only to be informed that both men are detectives – 'Sure, we was takin' her to stir!'. After the detectives have gone, Dick begins to have doubts. 'Those men didn't act or talk like detectives! I wonder?'

Two days later, the Travers Bridge collapses as threatened. $500,000 is demanded – or a third bridge will be destroyed in the same way. This time, Batman and Robin sweep into action and surprise the hoods, who are positioning a box-like contraption on the bridge. As the duo examine the box, the young woman who Dick saved from the 'detectives' reappears. She explains that the box is the work of her father, Doctor Vreekill, a scientist who has discovered a short-wave ray that can 'decompose the elements that make up steel.' He intends to use his invention to blackmail construction firms into paying protection money. His daughter tells

Bruce Wayne and Dick Grayson visit the New York World's fair, from *The New York World's Fair*, 1940.

Batman of her father's plans to 'free some dangerous prisoners tonight at the state prison so they may join his organization! Then he's going to destroy the half-finished Monarch building!' Batman and Robin foil the prisoners' escape, then race to the Monarch building site, where they battle with more hoods, before flying the Batplane to Doctor Vreekill's laboratory.

> Who?
>
> The Batman . . . and about to take you to jail!
>
> Jail? You'll never take me to jail! Never![39]

Vreekill electrocutes himself on some bare wires. 'Well, he saved the state the job' is Batman's verdict. The story concludes with another Batman and Robin endorsement of New York's World's Fair.

> It's got as many thrills as one of our adventures!
>
> And he's not kidding! If you want to see something that will not only educate you, but thrill you, by all means see the New York World's Fair.[40]

In its construction and organization, this text is typical of a certain kind of superhero narrative of the 1940s – historically, the period in which the genre was formulating rules and approaches which later artists and writers could obey or flout – but not ignore. The structure and preoccupations of this text are typical of the so-called Golden Age.

Batman and Robin expend considerable effort and risk themselves in unarmed combat against men with guns in defence of – what? One answer might be 'Law and order', but clearly a man and boy who have no official connection with the police force and operate in disguise and through the use of secret identities are not agents of the law in the same way as the heroes of (say) an Edgar Wallace novel. The splash panel at the beginning to the story comments:

> Wealth, lust for power, these are the roots of evil that tend to plant themselves in man's heart and mind. . . . crime, havoc and destruction, these are the fruits. Once again it remains for the Batman and Robin, the boy wonder, to pit their amazing skill against one who would become a king of crime . . . a king of evil . . .[41]

These words are positioned over the image of an enthusiastic Bruce and Dick arriving at the World's Fair, symbolic of rational and utopian values. Crime erupts into this ordered environment, and – significantly – crime against the fabric of the city, undertaken through the misappliance of science: Vreekill's machine that can 'decompose the elements that make up steel.' Though not quite a

Dr Vreekill is cornered and takes his own life, in *The New York World's Fair*. Bob Kane's circular panels punctuate the page. The shaping of the speech balloons and their organization on the page also controls the pacing of the narrative.

supervillain, Vreekill's bald head and functional costume signify him clearly as a 'mad scientist'. There is no exploration of the psychology that leads Vreekill to use his discovery for the pursuit of crime:

> With my machine I can become the most powerful man in the world! I can hold it as a club over those who deal in steel constructions.[42]

This is clearly not a sociological view of the roots of crime. The mythology underlying the text is that of the Old Testament, and, most specifically, the Temptation and Fall. Vreekill is a prototype for many 'Fallen' characters which Batman and other superheroes have encountered through the years – the Joker, Two-Face, Lex Luthor, Doctor Doom, Magneto, Ozymandias. All are corrupted by power, and power in the particular form of knowledge. 'Ye shall be as gods, knowing good and evil', promises the serpent in Genesis III. Barthes, in the essay 'Myth Today'[43] and elsewhere, has highlighted many of the ways in which mythology can be used to represent culture as nature, and thus 'explain' as natural and inevitable many of the social and political structures of our society. 'Batman and Robin visit the 1940 New York World's Fair' mythologizes the idea of crime, dramatizing the individual's criminal potential through the decisions taken from a position of power (i.e. knowledge). If history is to be understood as a progress towards Utopia, a significant tension can be adduced between superheroes (assisting this process) and villains (thwarting the Utopia builders, or 'those who deal in steel constructions').

This mythologizing of the dangers of scientific knowledge is one of the mainstream currents of science fiction, from *Frankenstein* through to the famous Spock/McCoy reason/conscience conflict in *Star Trek* (a conflict which is spuriously resolved by the *deus ex machina* of Kirk's overarching 'humanity', which embraces such contradictions and thereby resolves them.) However, the more radical split of knowledge and conscience which is signified by comic-book supervillains cannot be so easily reconciled within the confines of the genre. A villain such as the Joker continues year after year, story after story, sabotaging the social order in an endless treadmill of destruction, which Batman struggles to control and contain.

Such would be the 'preferred' reading of a text such as 'The World's Fair'. Clearly, a number of contradictory readings can be advanced. For example, certain oppositional readings identify with the personal exploitation of knowledge and power espoused by Dr Vreekill. In an early superhero text such as this, however, the difference between the preferred and oppositional readings remains clear-cut. The weight of moral decisions and their preferred interpretation are clearly inscribed in the construction of the narrative. Kane's art signals moments of moral decision very precisely, often by the use of a circular panel framing the character or the character's head. This is a narrative device akin to a film director's 'holding' on a close-up, but the tight circular story panel serves the additional function of breaking up the visual flow of the narrative, acting as a giant-sized full-stop. Such visual punctuation abstracts the contents of the panel from their context, a process which is helped on its way by the absence of any detailed backgrounds – although the panel in which Bruce and Dick agree to investigate the first bridge collapse shows both figures against a schematized New York skyline, the city they have pledged themselves to defend. The central conflict of the story is resolved in two circular panels on the last page. They are placed one above the other, although separated in narrative space by the two intervening panels that form the left-hand side of the bottom row. The upper circular panel shows Vreekill in the act of grabbing at the bare electric wire, destroyed by the forces he intended to exploit. The lower panel shows the triumphant Bruce and Dick, delivering their final homily on the virtues of the World's Fair. The reader is invited to participate, along with the story's heroes, in the alliance of knowledge and social order which the narrative has made visible.

2 Costumed Continuity

Costume functions as the crucial sign of super-heroism. It marks out heroes (and villains) from other characters who do not wear costumes. In this sense, costume functions as a uniform, binding together all super-beings and costumed characters in contrast to the non-costumed ordinary world. The appearance of a costumed character in a story will generate a specific set of expectations – a state of affairs which the writer and artist can work with or against, but which cannot be left wholly out of account.

The superhero's costume also proclaims his individuality. Costumes are a riot of different colours and designs; masked or unmasked, caped or capeless, bright or sombre colours, revealing or modest. Superheroines tend to reveal a lot more bare flesh than their male colleagues, but costume colour and other details vary across the board for both sexes. Costume is the sign of individual identity – a new identity, as the alter ego has been shed, if not actually hidden under a mask. The most cunning mask is no mask at all – as when a hero has a secret identity so unexpected or so well-contrived, such as Donald Blake/Thor or Clark Kent/Superman, that context is a sufficient alibi for the familiar face.

The conventions of superhero costume constitute a system of *langue* and *parole* – to use the terms first introduced by Saussure.[1] The *langue* (or language) is the structure of costume conventions, the rules that dictate the kind of costumes characters may wear. An individual costume is an example of *parole* – a specific utterance within this structured language of signs. Endless variety is possible within the compass of immediate understanding – a costume can be 'read' to indicate an individual hero's character or powers and (incidentally) as a signal that he is now operating in his superhero identity and may at any moment be involved in violent conflict with costumed villains.

The discourse implicit in superhero costumes is far from being an arbitrary set of conventions. Batman's dark, bat-like costume is one utterance within the code that elegantly speaks the proper range of associations: night, fear, the supernatural. It also suggests Batman's mode of operation: stealth, concealment, surprise. Iron Man's costume, by contrast, literally embodies his power: in his superpowered armour – which is also his identity-concealing costume – Tony Stark and other Iron Men have become invulnerable creatures of steel. Two functions are woven together: the role of the costume as a narrative device (giving Iron Man the powers he needs to fight villains) and its role as a sign of identity (to wear the costume is to become Iron Man). Individual stories explore this contrast between costume as a source of power and costume as a means of hiding identity, and the contrast between the suit and the man inside the suit has been complicated by the creation at various times of life-size models of Tony Stark ('Life Model Decoys') and empty suits of armour, which have on occasion turned on their creator.[2] The authentic Iron Man requires the right man in the right armoured suit. In a reflective moment, Tony Stark muses that:

> . . . After all these years you'd think the whole world would've put two and two together . . . and pieced out my dual identity! Thor knows it, as does Whitney, the Hogans, and Mike O'Brien. But Stark's history of heart trouble has kept everyone else off the track! But then, why should most people even care? They've got other things on their minds . . . like the rising cost of living . . . neutron bombs . . . braces for their kids teeth! Why should Joe or Jane America care who . . . or what . . . is inside this metal suit . . . as long as Iron Man gets the job done? As long as I risk my life to bring them peace of mind?[3]

The five panels of Carmine Infantino's artwork that comprise this soliloquy are a fine example of superhero sequential art, despite the fact that almost no action takes place. Panel 1 presents the figure of Iron Man in silhouette, against a dark and brooding background of the corridors of Stark International, recently devastated in a battle with the villainous Midas. Iron Man's silhouette ripples with muscles, despite the fact that the visible torso is his metal armour, not flesh. The gauntlets, boots and 'swimming trunks' of the armour add to the impression of a nude man with a robot's head. The figure dominates the panel, purposeful in its attitude, yet subsumed by the shadowy chiaroscuro background – a robot made flesh.

Panel 2 shows Iron Man's torso and head emerging through a door on which the word 'Stark' can be deciphered. Iron Man is rendered in colour, and the open door's edge splits the panel in half, placing the robotlike head and torso of Iron Man rather weakly in the bottom right hand corner, less human but far more vulnerable than in panel 1. The name on the door and the robot-like torso emerging underline the Stark/Iron Man duality.

Panel 3 synthesizes these two views of our hero. A three-quarter view from behind emphasizes both human strength (metallic muscles) and robot form (angular shoulders, smooth head). The moody shadows and Iron Man's stance, staring through a blank window, seemingly at nothing, echo the bleak sentiment of the words 'But why should most people even care? . . .'

Panel 4 takes the reader in far closer. In profile, Stark presses the button that lifts off his face-mask ('Klik' is the added sound effect).

***Iron Man* 108, page 11. The man behind the mask. *Iron Man* 108, © Marvel Entertainment Group, Inc. 1977.**

Stark's face remains shadowed by the mask, which, lifted up, seems to resemble the theatrical mask of tragedy. Panel 5 completes this page-long sequence. Stark's face, mask flipped up, is split in half by the panel border: half a face, and half a mask, foreshortened and almost 'unreadable'. But just as central to the panel as the visible half of Stark's face is the enhanced hearing equipment mounted on the side of his head – which is robot-like. Moreover, behind the human features in the foreground, framed as they are by the metal of Iron Man's helmet, we can see the shadow thrown behind from the window last seen in panel 3. The shadowed profile is wholly sharp and robotic, a smoothly curving outline. This black shadow, stalking behind, suggests the burden the heroic identity places on Stark, denying him 'Peace, that I, myself, have never known!' The melodrama of the words is underscored and undercut throughout the page by the narrative discourse of the artwork, which embodies no 'action' other than exploration of the hero's character, or split personality. Furthermore, even at moments of violent conflict with villains, Iron Man remains two persons in one. The man inside the suit is repeatedly called upon to earn his right to the powers which the suit's technology confer. ('It's not the suit but the man inside it'). This 'earning' of the suit's powers usually involves the use of the special 'extra effort' discussed on page 41.

Costume is more than a disguise: it functions as a sign for the inward process of character development. The Wasp, Iron Man's one-time colleague in Marvel's Avengers superhero team, brings a different kind of rhetoric to her repeated changes of costume – by virtue of her alter-ego Janet Van Dyne, socialite and fashion designer. Unlike heroes who slug their way through fight after fight in the same costume, the Wasp has sported a bewildering variety of outfits since her first appearance in 1962. In part, the Wasp's submission to the dialectic of fashion is an expression of her femininity – her costumes are changed purely for the sake of appearances. Yet, as the Wasp/Janet Van Dyne dual identity is not a secret one, the frequent changes of costume successfully blur the boundaries between fashion designer and superheroine.[4]

Contrastingly, the Wasp's one-time lover and husband Henry Pym (variously known in costume as Ant-Man, Giant Man and Yellowjacket)[5] underwent his quick-change costume variations as part of a protracted effort to define and refine his own powers and superpowered identity. Ultimately, Pym's problem centred on justifying his place in a super-team full of more powerful and more charismatic super-characters (Thor, Iron Man, Captain America, to name but three). And Pym's failure to find any definitive version of his costume placed him firmly in the ranks of secondary or back-up characters, unworthy of their own comic-book and therefore only viable as part of a superhero social grouping such as The Avengers. To change the costume of Captain America or Batman would mean redefining a precise iconographic configuration. Changing the costume of the Wasp or Yellowjacket, or the bow-and-arrow Avenger Hawkeye, can be happily placed within the ambit of character development. Clearly, the costume of any individual hero or heroine must obey both the rules of langue and parole; i.e. it must be recognizably an utterance within the rules of the costume system, and should – within the compass of those rules – make a formal statement about the hero's personality and character development.

Even texts such as *The Dark Knight Returns* and *Watchmen* – which make playful intertextual allusions to other superhero comics – do not by and large break the rules of the costume langue and parole system. Rather, they play a knowing set of variations with the audience's established pattern of responses, based on a shared knowledge of the rules of costume, and what might be said to constitute a violation of these rules. Thus, in *The Dark Knight Returns*, Frank Miller introduces along with his middle-aged Batman a middle-aged Green Arrow, ready to help Batman in his final showdown with Superman. But Green Arrow is never explicitly identified as being the Green Arrow from current DC storylines. His appearance, bow, and use of his alter-ego name Oliver are enough to adduce an intertextual input of Green Arrow's status as a modern day Robin Hood, and his long-standing opposition to the 'establishment' political values embraced by Superman in this text and in general.[6]

Likewise, in *Watchmen*, the deconstruction of costumed superhero values is pursued as part of the deconstruction of the costumes themselves. Superhero costumes are either sexless, denying the humanity of the hero within, or garments of great erotic significance. Doctor Manhattan, omnipotent super-being, spends his 25 year career shedding piece-by-piece the all-enveloping costume provided for him by the US government. At the end of the book he chooses to go naked. And the semiotic function of superhero costume can be unpicked in more ways than one. Nite Owl reveals the fetishism implicit in the design of most superhero costumes, during his exceptionally well-realized first sexual encounter with Laurie Juszpeczyk, the Silk Spectre:

Dan, was tonight good? Did you like it?

Costume as fetish: Nite Owl dreams of Laurie Juszpeczyk and the Twilight Lady, from *Watchmen* 7, page 16.

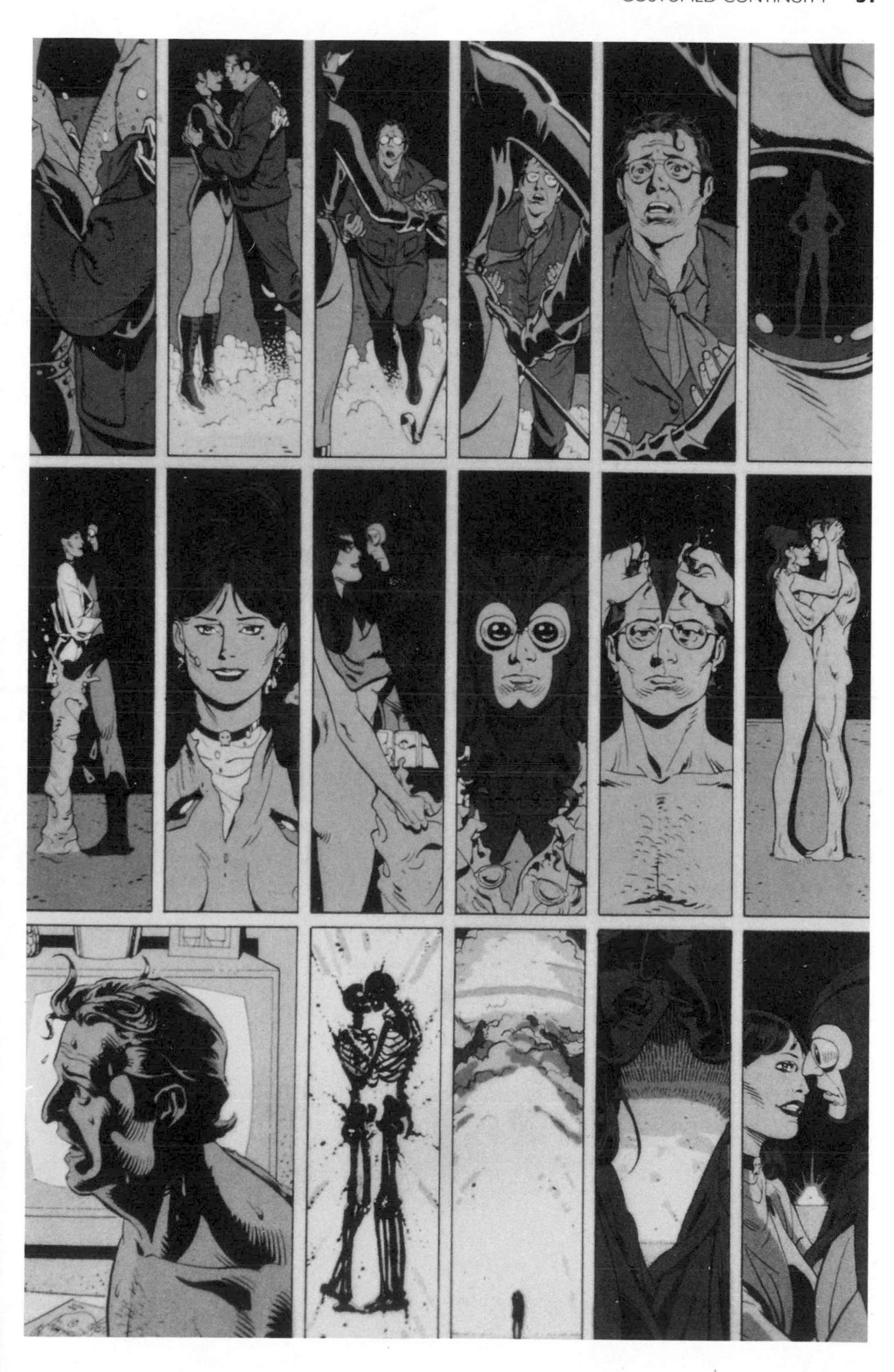

> Uh-huh.
>
> Did the costumes make it good? Dan . . .?
>
> Yeah. Yeah, I guess the costumes had something to do with it. It just feels strange, you know? To come out and admit that to somebody. To come out of the closet.[7]

These panels pull out of the closet a subtext present since the very first superhero story. Superman's prowess in defeating Butch Matson is only the earliest of many examples of the sudden virility and sex-appeal gained when a character changes 'into costume'. What if the costume were more than just a sign of the inner change from wimp to Superman? What if the costume itself were the sexual fetish and the source of sexual power?

Out of costume, Dan (Nite Owl) Dreiberg is a rather sleazy descendant of the Clark Kent dynasty. His portly figure, macintosh and unsuccessfully quiffed hairstyle almost put him in the Dirty Old Man category that might be drawn to real-life superheroines in fetishistic costumes. Nite Owl is partly modelled on the old Charlton comics character the Blue Beetle (as Rorschach in *Watchmen* is partially based on the Question).[8] But Nite Owl's *modus operandi*, his totemic relationship with a flying creature of the night, his lack of superpowers and reliance on fitness and gadgetry – all these suggest an affiliation with and reference to a much more familiar superhero: the Batman. The costumes of both are dark in colour, suggesting the flying night creatures from which they derive – yet also include the rubber or leather masks associated with rapists and serial sex killers. Nite Owl's fascination with sado-masochism and fetishistic clothing is made explicit in *Watchmen* 7. Laurie Juszpeczyk, poking about in her boyfriend's basement HQ, comes across a signed portrait of a leather-clad dominatrix figure with the inscription 'From one "Night Bird" to Another. The Twilight Lady.'

> That? Oh, that isn't anybody. It's just this vice queen I put away back in '68. Called herself Dusk Woman or something.
>
> 'The Twilight Lady.' She sent you her picture?
>
> Yeah, well, I guess she had some sort of fixation. She was a very sick woman. I keep meaning to throw that picture away, but you know how it is . . .
>
> Mmm . . .[9]

Subsequently, after an unsuccessful attempt to consumate his rela-

Costume as fetish (2): Nite Owl comes out of the closet. *Watchmen* 7, page 28.

I THOUGHT YOU'D QUIT, LAURIE.
DANGEROUS HABITS, REMEMBER?
THERE'S NO SUCH THING AS QUITTING. JUST SOMETIMES THERE'S A LONGER PAUSE BETWEEN RELAPSES, RIGHT?
UH-HUH.
DAN, WAS TONIGHT GOOD? DID YOU LIKE IT?
DID THE COSTUMES MAKE IT GOOD?
DAN...?
YEAH.
YEAH, I GUESS THE COSTUMES HAD SOMETHING TO DO WITH IT. IT JUST FEELS STRANGE, YOU KNOW? TO COME OUT AND ADMIT THAT TO SOMEBODY.
TO COME OUT OF THE CLOSET.
DOES IT FEEL GOOD?
OH, YES. JESUS, YES.
I FEEL SO CONFIDENT. IT'S LIKE I'M ON FIRE. AND ALL THE MASK KILLERS, ALL THE WARS IN THE WORLD, THEY'RE JUST CASES--JUST PROBLEMS TO SOLVE.
HMMM. Y'KNOW, YOU SOUND REAL PASSIONATE. I DIDN'T KNOW YOU COULD SMOLDER.
I'D HOPED TONIGHT MIGHT WAKE SOMETHING INSIDE YOU, BUT IT SOUNDS LIKE IT'S AWOKEN WITH AN APPETITE.
YOU'RE RIGHT. IT HAS. A BIG APPETITE.
MMMMM. INSATIABLE, HUH? WELL, I'M OPEN TO SUGGESTIONS. WHAT SHALL WE DO NEXT?
I'VE BEEN THINKING ABOUT THAT, AND I FEEL WE HAVE CERTAIN OBLIGATIONS TO OUR FRATERNITY.
I THINK WE SHOULD SPRING RORSCHACH.
WHAT?
28
"I am a brother to dragons, and a companion to owls. My skin is black upon me, and my bones are burned with heat."
JOB chapter 30, verses 29-30

tionship with Laurie, Nite Owl dreams of the black-leather clad Twilight Lady, complete with whip, who rips away his clothes and then his flesh to reveal the superhero costume underneath. Nite Owl rips away Twilight Lady's costume to uncover her nude body and then the costumed body of Laurie Juszpeczyk. The stripping away of sexual imagery is terminated by a nuclear explosion, portrayed in the often-reproduced image (on T-shirts, and elsewhere) of two skeletons embracing against a background of nuclear apocalypse.[10]

One of the many remarkable aspects of *Watchmen* is the deft way in which Moore and Gibbons deploy multi-layered intertextual themes from the entire canon of superhero comics. A fully engaged reading of *Watchmen* demands a broad familiarity with the overall preoccupations of the genre throughout its history. Textually, *Watchmen* functions as a critical response to the accumulation of over 50 years of superhero stories. These at all times underpin the text's strategy of unmasking the subtexts behind conventional superhero narratives – such as the amalgam of sexual fear and desire signified by male and female superhero costumes.

The appearance and costume of the original superheroine, Wonder Woman, was developed as a frank appeal to male fantasies of sexual domination, as disingenuously set forth by Wonder Woman's creator, psychologist Dr William Moulton Marston:

> Give them an alluring woman stronger than themselves to submit to and they'll be proud to be her willing slaves![11]

Wonder Woman's inconography of whips and chains became the jumping-off point for the sub-genre of 'Good Girl' art – superheroines as exciting for their looks as for their villain-bashing exploits. Good Girl superheroines of the 1940s operated in the wider context of the Vargas pin-up girls, the Just Jane cartoons and sweethearts of the forces such as Betty Grable and Rita Hayworth. Good Girl art takes the signs of pornographic discourse (whips, chains, spiked heels, beautiful but blank faces) and integrates them into the context of non-pornographic story structures. In this way, the sign of pornography (never explicitly delivered) comes to stand in for an entire pornographic subtext, a series of blanks which readers remain free to fill in for themselves. And it is within the neo-pornographic texts of Good Girl art that the distinctions between costumed heroes and villains can first be seen to break down, a change that in turn influenced mainstream superhero comics. Batman's arch-enemy the Catwoman is not so different in looks and style from Good Girl heroines such as Matt Baker's Phantom Lady or Tarpe Mills' Miss Fury.[12]

This blurring of the boundaries between heroine and villainess

The She-Hulk gets ready for a date, in the 1985 *She-Hulk Graphic Novel.* 'I'm six foot seven tall and bright green—people are going to stare however I dress.' *The Sensational She-Hulk,* © Marvel Entertainment Group, Inc. 1985, 1990.

YOU HEARD ME. NOW DROP 'EM...
...OR YOU CAN BURY YOUR BOYFRIEND AT WOUNDED KNEE...
SHE-HULK, DON'T! YOUR LEGAL RIGHTS...
...DON'T COUNT FOR MUCH AROUND THESE PARTS, I EXPECT. WELL... I CAN ALWAYS WRITE A NASTY NOTE TO MY CONGRESSMAN LATER.
S'ALL RIGHT, LOVER. NOTHING WORTH YOUR GETTING VENTILATED FOR.
FUNNY THING, THOUGH. I REMEMBER WHEN SHIELD WAS THE GOOD GUYS.
I GUESS THAT'S THE TROUBLE WITH PARA-MILITARY SPY GROUPS.
THEY TEND TO START OUT AS THE SECRET SERVICE, AND END UP AS THE K.G.B.
SEEMS LIKE IT'S ALL BEEN DOWNHILL SINCE THEY CANCELED "THE MAN FROM U.N.C.L.E."
OKAY, BRIGHT-BOYS, NOW WHAT?
MAYBE YOU'D LIKE ME TO JUMP ROPE FOR YOU?

should be seen in the context of contemporary Hollywood female leads such as Barbara Stanwyck and Veronica Lake – a tough, fascinating and (for the male victims) even menacing construct of sexuality, never hitherto as openly acknowledged in the discourse of popular culture. The costumed heroine may be frankly the object of sexual attraction, and therefore (for many male readers) will constitute the object of their gaze, as well as the subject or protagonist through which they engage with the action of the text. So, whilst for the superhero the transformation into costume can best be achieved with something as instantaneous as Billy Batson's 'Shazam', which calls forth the invincible Captain Marvel, for the superheroine the process can (at least potentially) be viewed as the performance of an uncompleted striptease. And thus the (male) reader is called upon to 'read' both heroines and villainesses as objects of desire – 'good girls' and 'bad girls' maybe, but objects of the same rhetorical logic.[13]

Costume creates a community between its wearers. The costumed superheroes generate their own particular world – a world which starts at the point where our own familiar world leaves off. All the additions to the familiar world are extraordinary ones: invasions from space, mutations, master criminals, the supernatural. It's our own world made stranger and more robust to fit the stature of the larger-than-life hero.

The creation of the superhero's world becomes more complex when we turn to the genre of the 'team' superhero comic – the comic in which the protagonists are not individual heroes but a team, whose actual membership may vary from one issue to the next. These titles date back to the Golden Age, starting with *All Star Comics* 3 (1940) and the first meeting of the Justice Society of America – the first superhero team.

Clearly, there are good commercial reasons for the team or group superhero comic, just as there are sound commercial reasons for team-ups and crossovers between individual titles. Extra superheroes, especially popular ones mixed with the new or the less popular, mean extra sales. *The Brave and the Bold* has been featuring Batman teamed with less illustrious heroes since 1966.[14] However, the textual consequences of the team-up or group comic are worthy of separate consideration. Close links are established between characters and groups of characters. With enough team-ups

The night out goes wrong. She-Hulk is strip-searched by corrupt SHIELD agents while her boyfriend has a gun held to his head. The reader is manoevered into the position of voyeur. *The Sensational She-Hulk*, © Marvel Entertainment Group, Inc. 1985, 1990.

(and there have been plenty) links are established between all the costumed characters published by a particular company.

This intertextuality, forming in total the 'Marvel Universe' and 'DC Universe', is the feature of superhero comics that most often surprises those who are not regular readers. Conversely, 'continuity' – as it is always known – forms the most crucial aspect of enjoyment for the committed fans. Continuity is a familiar idea for all followers of soap opera, but, as practised by the two major superhero publishers, continuity is of an order of complexity beyond anything to which the television audience has become accustomed. An appreciation of the importance of continuity is an essential prerequisite to a fully-engaged reading of superhero comics, especially those published post Silver Age. The more comics published, the more continuity there is to cohere. So much so that, in 1986, DC organized the *Crisis on Infinite Earths* story to reconstruct their continuity and wipe away some of the highly constricting backgrounds and characterizations that had emerged over nearly 50 years of publishing.[15] After this convulsion, several key titles, including *Superman* and *The Flash*, started all over again from issue No. 1.

In practice, fans tend to conflate several different types of intertextuality when using the word 'continuity'. Picking these meanings apart, it becomes possible to address some of the different levels at which the pleasure of continuity has become an expected and integral part of the pleasure of the superhero narrative.

1. Serial continuity

This is the same kind of continuity that is preserved (or not, as the case may be) in TV soaps. The back-story of a soap, comprising all the episodes previously screened, with their explicit or implied content, needs to remain consistent with the current storyline as it develops.

This is more of a challenge for the writer of comics, who works in an art-form which is far less ephemeral than television. Any fans worth their salt will be in possession of a pile of back-issues against which to check any current plot development which seems to violate any previous storyline. And the writers are sometimes caught out. At such a juncture their role (or the editor's role) is to save the day be conjuring up an explanation which smooths over the faux-pas and restores continuity. Sometimes this may not be possible, in which case the editors may frankly admit the error – impossible to imagine in the non-interactive world of TV soaps!

***Animal Man* 23, page 14 (1990). Characters from potential parallel worlds in the discontinued DC continuity (post *Crisis on Infinite Earths*) seek revenge for their annihilation.**

In the 1960s, Stan Lee at Marvel invented the non-existent 'no-prize' for fans who pointed out inexplicable blunders and gaps in continuity. A recent controversy over continuity involved the canonical status of *The Dark Knight Returns*: did this story of Batman's middle age form a part of DC's *Batman* continuity? In other words, would the monthly development of storylines in *Batman* and *Detective Comics* move towards the scenario depicted in *Dark Knight*? As a side-swipe at this kind of obsession with continuity, Alan Moore chose to preface his Superman two-parter 'Whatever Happened to the Man of Tomorrow?' with the caveat 'This is an IMAGINARY STORY (which may never happen, but then again may) about a perfect man who came from the sky and did only good . . . This is an IMAGINARY STORY . . . aren't they all?'[16]

2. Hierarchical continuity

This depends for its appreciation on an intertextual reading of several superhero comics – ultimately on the entire Marvel or DC line. At its most straightforward, hierarchical continuity implies that if superhero A defeats supervillain B in one comic and superhero C is defeated by supervillain B in another comic, then (assuming no other changes to continuity, such as one of the characters gaining or losing powers) superhero A is stronger than superhero C and should be able to defeat him in a head-to-head combat. This sort of situation regularly arises, and from the myriad meetings and conflicts between heroes and villains, heroes and other heroes, and even villains versus villains, an overall hierarchy of superbeings is continuously shaped and redefined. Characters such as Superman or Thor are at the top of this 'pecking order' and others such as Batman and Daredevil somewhere near the bottom.

It is important to note, however, that this 'squash ladder' hierarchy is merely a table of physical strength and fighting ability, and is quite separate from any league table that may exist of nobility, heroism, or indeed popularity with the readership. For example, the positioning of Batman and Daredevil near the bottom of the DC and Marvel hierarchies of strength in no way prevents them from being two of the most popular and enduring superheroes of all time. Batman, Daredevil and Captain America – all of them effectively non-superpowered – are among the most highly-regarded heroes of the DC and Marvel universes. Highly regarded, that is, by other superheroes. Superman has regularly teamed with Batman, despite their almost preposterous imbalance of strength and physical powers. Thor has regularly fought in *The Avengers* alongside Captain America – a Norse god alongside a highly-trained and agile human being. The negotiation of a character's heroism (or villainy) is fleshed out, as in all narrative, by the examination of moral choices made under pressure.

The pressure of combat also forces from heroes the quality which sums up the moral nature of the superhero: the 'extra effort'. No battle is ever won easily – at least, not in a properly constructed superhero narrative. A story where the hero blasts the villain with his superior powers is not a story worthy of the name. What the reader is generally looking for is the application of the extra effort, the moral determination to go on fighting even when apparently beaten. The moment of the extra effort, and the soul searching that is conducted to make it possible, are the key moments of most superhero narratives, and far more significant in terms of character development than all the acrobatic and artistic slugging and atomic, psychic, or electromagnetic zapping that comprises the progress of the fights themselves.

The hierarchy and structural continuity of the DC or Marvel line also highlights the emblematic function of superhero and supervillain costumes. Costumed characters all participate in the hierarchy of powers to some degree, whether those powers are used for good or evil. Non-costumed characters aren't involved in the hierarchy – even such major characters as Commissioner Gordon or Daredevil's friend and business partner Foggy Nelson. Likewise outside the hierarchy of powers are the police and non-costumed hoods, faceless thugs who seem almost interchangeable followers of any villain in town. *Avengers* 195–197 examines the sources of this seemingly unlimited supply of non-costumed hired hoods in the Marvel Universe, and uncovers a sinister training school under the command of the Taskmaster, a superpowered and costumed villain.

3. Structural continuity

Serial continuity, which is diachronic (it develops over time), and hierarchical continuity, which is synchronic (the state of affairs at a given moment), combine to produce structural continuity, which is, in short, the entire contents of the DC or Marvel universes. However, structural continuity embraces more than the sum total of all the stories and canonical interactions between superheroes, villains, and the supporting casts. Structural continuity also embraces those elements of the real world which are contained within the fictional universe of the superheroes, and (for the truly committed) actions which are not recorded in any specific text, but inescapably implied by continuity. (For example: what was the name of Superman's grandfather? We have never been told – but continuity implies that such a person must exist and could be drawn into the storyline at

***Superman versus Muhammad Ali,* 1978. Everything in the real world also exists in continuity. The faces in the crowd are all celebrities, DC artists and writers, or characters within DC continuity: the fictional world contains its own creators.**

any point, i.e. become a fixed part of continuity from that point onwards.)

If superheroes are to have any claim at all to be considered the bearers of a 'modern mythology' and in some ways comparable to the pantheons of Greek or Native American or Norse mythology, then this extra-textual continuity is a vital key to the way in which the mythology of comic books is articulated in the mind of the reader. The ideal fan is capable of envisaging an ideal DC or Marvel metatext: a summation of all existing texts plus all the gaps which those texts have left unspecified. This metatext, however, can never exist in any definite form, because

1. No fan has in practice ever read every single canonical DC or Marvel title (though some come closer than one has any right to expect).

2. New canonical texts are being added every month. Any definitive metatextual resolution is therefore indefinitely postponed. That is to say, the DC or Marvel universe is not finally defined until some future date when superhero texts cease to be published. In the meantime, new texts must be made sense of within continuity, or discarded as non-canonical.

The process is analogous to example of the theory advanced in T.S. Eliot's 'Tradition and the Individual Talent':

> what happens when a new work of art is created is something that happens simultaneously to all the works of art which preceded it. The existing monuments form an ideal order among themselves, which is modified by the introduction of the new (the really new) work of art among them. The existing order is complete before the new work arrives; for order to persist after the supervention of novelty, the whole existing order must be, if ever so slightly, altered . . .[17]

The discarding of texts that can't be fitted into the continuity can take two different forms. Some texts – such as the 1960s Batman television series – were never intended to form part of the overall Batman DC continuity, and fans have no problem separating these texts from the structure of continuity and enjoying them in isolation from the canonical works. Their use of a different medium and their unified, campy tone distance the TV shows sufficiently to permit them to operate in their own continuum.

Other texts, clearly intended to become canonical when first published, can become problematical over a period of time. Captain America, for example, was created by Jack Kirby in 1941, as America's first super soldier in the battle against the Nazis. The scientific formula responsible was lost immediately after giving scrawny Steve

Rogers his own (modest) superpowers – Captain America remained a uniquely endowed super-soldier. With the decline in popularity of costumed superheroes in the late 1940s, Captain America's title folded and, apart from a brief revival in 1954, the character wasn't seen in action again until Stan Lee introduced him into *The Avengers* in 1964.[18] A narrative device was required to explain how Steve Rogers could still be the same age over 20 years after he first swallowed the super-soldier serum. This problem was solved by having Captain America dug out of a block of ice in which he had been frozen since the end of the war (ignoring those 1954 appearances). The Avengers thawed out Cap and found him to be as good as new – a costumed Rip van Winkle. He remains to this day in the limbo of 25–30 years of age into which most adult superheroes settle.

But since 1964, time has continued to roll on. The time that has passed since 1964 has been telescoped into continuity, which is openly non-historical and doesn't move forward at any set pace. But the period of time when Captain America was out of the continuity altogether is treated as historical – the time when no Captain America stories were being published, or at least none which are now regarded as canonical. Yet Steve Rogers/Captain America has now remained 'frozen' in his late twenties for far longer than he was literally frozen in the ice.[19] Clearly, intertextual and metatextual continuity create a subsidiary world in which the process of time can be kept under control. While this process does not exactly abolish history from superhero comics, it does divorce the superheroes lives from their historical context. For example, the early Fantastic Four stories were written against the background of the Cold War and the Cuba Missile Crisis,[20] but to anchor these events into continuity would mean that the characters must have aged by 30 years since the inception of the comic. Thus the demands of continuity work against the use of frankly political themes, or at least their literal treatment.

Another temporal paradox was neatly fitted into DC's continuity from the start of the Silver Age (1956). Most of the characters revived from the Golden Age – The Flash, The Green Lantern, The Atom, Hawkman and so on – might be expected to have grown older in the intervening years since the 1940s. This problem was solved by creating a series of alternate earths – Earth One, Earth Two and so on – on which the major characters could exist simultaneously at different stages of their lives. Thus the Golden Age Bruce Wayne could continue to exist as a semi-retired middle-aged individual on Earth One, while on Earth Two a younger, thirtysomething Bruce Wayne could carry on as a fully active Batman. This arrangement carried the additional refinement of placing the reader inside the infinite worlds defined within the compass of continuity. Our familiar world with no superheroes became just one of the many alternative earths generated by the mechanism of DC continuity. This last possibility has been taken advantage of in several stories, including the Alan Brennert/Dick Giordano collaboration 'To Kill a Legend', from 1981's *Detective Comics* 500, discussed in detail in the following chapter. The continuity structures which allowed such stories to take place were dismantled in the 1986 *Crisis on Infinite Earths* storyline.

Continuity, and above all metatextual structural continuity, is the strategy through which superhero texts most clearly operate as myths. Continuity provides the interaction with the audience which characterizes mythological discourse: myths, like music, have been characterized by Levi-Strauss as 'machines for the suppression of time', the contemplation of the unity being more important than any suspense engendered over the outcome. It is through such devices that the superhero comic provides a mythological model of society's simultaneous unity and plurality – '*e pluribus unum*', as the US Constitutional motto has it.[21] Moreover, both music and myth depend for their articulation on the co-operation and participation of the audience:

> . . . what the individual listener understands when he hears a myth or a piece of music is in many ways personal to himself – it is the receiver who decides what the message is.[22]

This is true of the readership of superhero comics in a very practical sense. The continuity of an individual character, and the relationship of that character with the entire 'universe' which they inhabit, provides a guarantee of the authenticity of each individual story. The continuity is a *langue* in which each particular story is an utterance.

Fans clearly read the structure of the superhero metatexts in this way. Suggestions for new stories which evince a potential to combine hitherto uncombined elements of the metatext make up one of the most frequent kind of correspondence in the letter columns of superhero comics. The following letter was published in *Fantastic Four* 87 (June 1969), at the height of Marvel and Stan Lee's elevation of their characters into a seamless and continuous mythology:

> Dear Stan [Lee] and Jack [Kirby]
> Shortly after my first letter was published in FF78 with my theory on the Torch's flame: namely, coating his fireproof body and clothing with 'photo-chemical endo-thermal reaction utilizing quasi-volatile gasio-solids and mentally dominated oxygen-rich plasmas (bet you

> never thought you'd see THAT again)! A brief flurry of controversy stirred Marveldom Assembled, and as one who never leaves well enough alone, I return, unconquered. It has been suggested that the Torch and the X-Man Iceman become their respective elements, fire and ice. Skipping over the problems of making such creatures live, what happens when some baddy douses Johnny or leaves Bobby in the oven too long? They return to normal. If the fire-and-ice theory were true, I know a certain comics group that would be looking for two new superheroes. While on subjects pyric and glacial, I have a plot suggestion. How about teaming up these temperature twins? Extreme cold and heat, alternately applied, should break down anything but one of Galactus' photon forcefields . . . As I see it, the time is ripe for another stunning two-part-story-in-one-month bonanza like the epoch-making battle between the X-Men and the Avengers. You could start off with Cerebro picking up Junior's brainwave pattern, along with the gadgets used by Magneto, Doc Doom, and/or the Wizard. Lead the plot into some wild team-ups such as: Torch-Iceman, Beast-Thing, Invisible Girl-Marvel Girl-Crystal, Cyclops-Reed-Angel! 'Til Junior trips over his long white beard, MAKE MINE MARVEL!
>
> Tom Zmudzinski, 463 Cumberland-B, Univ. of Maryland College Park, Md.[23]

The writer of the letter is a college student. He has written before to the *Fantastic Four* letter column, and sees his previous letter and the current one as being part of a developing debate between *Fantastic Four* readers. The purpose of the first part of the letter is to restate the writer's own 'scientific theory' accounting for the superpowers of two Marvel characters: the Human Torch of the Fantastic Four and the Iceman, an original member of the X-Men. After restating this (bogus) scientific explanation of the Torch's powers, he proceeds to refute a more openly magical explanation offered by another reader.

The Torch and the Iceman, with their complimentary and elemental powers, strike Zmudzinski as affording a perfect opportunity for a team-up. This initial suggestion generates a whole set of accompanying ideas, which almost become a text in their own right: 'the time is right for a stunning two-part-story-in-one-month bonanza' – which appreciates the virtues of correct timing as well as the realities of serial publication. In other words, the reader's suggestion is a practical one on the intersecting planes of both textual continuity and commercial publishing. Such an X-Men/Fantastic Four team-up would be a crossover story, and would probably have been undertaken in the way Zmudzinski suggests – simultaneous publication of monthly issues of the *X-Men* and *Fantastic Four* that form a single, two-part story. (In fact, the proposed team-up never happened). The potential utterance is within the *langue* of continuity, and is furthermore given some fairly detailed fleshing-out – 'lead the plot into some wild team-ups'.

The Torch has baffling and apparently inexplicable powers, but as those powers are real within the given structure of continuity, the job is not to make those powers less baffling, but to explain them within the parameters which continuity allows. Yet continuity is also something malleable, and constantly in the process of being shaped by the collective forces of artists, writers, editors, and even the critical voices of the fans. Meanwhile, there are limitless opportunities for small-scale sub-creation in areas of the DC or Marvel universes, where fans can exercise their ingenuity and imagination within the governing discipline of overall continuity. And – it hardly needs to be said – several of the most frequent letter-writing fans have progressed to become artists, writers, editors and publishers in their own right.[24]

This touches on a significant aspect of comic-book publication which must be measured against the demands of continuity: the fan-following for particular writers or (more commonly) artists. The chief superhero artists constitute a hierarchy which exists independently of intertextual continuity. Bob Kane, Jack Kirby, Dick Giordano, Neal Adams, Gene Colan, John Byrne, Jim Steranko, Frank Miller, Bill Sienkiewicz, Brian Bolland, Dave Gibbons: these and many other artists have been the stars of individual titles and projects as much as the characters they portray. Many have oscillated between DC and Marvel, and worked at various times outside the comic field altogether. Certain writers have also enjoyed a similar status – writer-artists such as Miller or Byrne or Jim Starlin – as well as writers pure and simple such as Roy Thomas, Stan Lee, Chris Claremont, Len Wein and, most notably, Alan Moore. The comings and goings of major artists and writers on key titles are events in their own right, existing parallel to the progress of continuity, and yet able to affect the seamless intertextual fiction in a premeditated way. Thus John Byrne's arrival at *Superman* or Moore's scripting of *Swamp Thing* are decisive events in the evolution of those particular characters. We can legitimately speak of Byrne's Superman or Messner-Loebs' Flash as being different from other writer's conceptions of these characters, without negating the assumption of continuity on which the prosecution of the continuing saga rests.[25]

This tendency might seem to work against the successful maintenance of continuity – if, every year or two, Batman or Daredevil are reconstituted as 'Adams' Batman' or 'Miller's Daredevil'. In fact, the reverse seems to be the case. Because there is such a focused determination among writers and fans that continuity shall be kept up at all costs, there always remains plenty of room for the reinterpretation of consistent facts within the style of a particular creative team. One element in the character's myth (for example, the character's origin) can be used to generate a potentially unlimited number of texts, even texts which seem to 'tell the same story'. Continuity implies an agreed body of material which exists independently of any specific text – analagous perhaps to the way in which different medieval poets could retell the 'Matter of Britain' before Malory attempted a systematizing of the Arthurian 'continuity' in the *Morte D'Arthur*.

The fixed points which are reinterpreted with most regularity are the origins of major characters – generally heroes, sometimes villains. It has almost become a custom that, when taking over a new assignment, a new writer/artist team will be expected to have a shot at redefining a character's origin story. The fan expectations from such an event might be summed up as follows:

1. The retelling of the origin will bring some new aspect of the character to light.

2. The new creative team will use the stamp of its own creative style as a governing element in the reinterpretation of the character.

3. Whatever new material is created and whatever new connections are made between existing plot-lines, continuity will be seen to be preserved.

A new hero or villain isn't around for long before demands begin from the fans for the 'origin story'. The fixing of a character's origin ties down an initial, all-important moment of transformation – for example: how did a previously normal human being acquire superpowers and/or a secret identity? This cardinal moment of transformation, where the everyday world is chosen to intersect with the superhero metatext, underwrites all of a character's subsequent transformations and adventures. Once an individual has been inducted into the superhero continuity, the whole metatext lies open for adventure and exploration. The world within the atom and the planets of the Kree or Bizarros lie within the realm of appropriate textual utterances.[26] Daredevil may specialize in cleaning up crime from the streets of New York but (like the equally non-superpowered Batman) he has also found the time to battle invaders from distant galaxies and demons from parallel dimensions. Conversely, the nearly-omnipotent Thor and Superman have often been seen to intervene in muggings. A superhero has free passage to any part of the continuity.

Origin and costume are thus closely linked in character development. Generally speaking, a hero's costume (the sign of superpowers) is linked in some (permanently visible) way with his origin. Superman's costume is woven from the blanket which swaddled him on his journey from Krypton to Earth. Tony Stark's Iron Man costume began as an extension of the chest plate needed to aid his diseased heart. Spider-Man's costume portrays and externalizes Peter Parker's spider-like and spider-derived powers. Captain America's red, white and blue appropriate and mobilize the patriotic emotions attendant on the character's creation. The Spectre, who really is a ghost, combines the morphology of the superhero costume – cape, hood, underpants worn on the outside – with the spectral colours of green and white. Green Arrow's costume, on the other hand, uses the colour green to summon up the legend of Robin Hood. Carrie Kelly, the female Robin of Frank Miller's *The Dark Knight Returns*, wears a similar costume to the three Robins featured so far in Batman's career: Dick Grayson, Jason Todd and Tim Drake. The most enduring villains likewise have costumes which are perfectly emblematic of their character and capabilities. And it is through costume and origin that the supervillains define themselves as worthy and legitimate opponents of superheroes.

Historically, this took a while to sort itself out. A very early 'supervillain', such as the Monk/Vampire (*Detective Comics* 31–32, 1939) is not properly distinguished from the order from which he takes his name. That is to say, he might simply be a monk, not a costumed character who has taken that name and its concomitant attributes. The Monk does not belong to the same world as the hero he opposes, despite the elegant structural opposition of his capabilities, powers and inclinations (withdrawal, bat-like powers) with those of Batman. The Monk addresses Batman (and therefore the reader) with a complete absence of familiarity:

> Rash mortal . . . To dare face the power of the Monk . . .[27]

This distancing of the villain from the hero began to disappear in the 1940s, as regularly recurring villains became the strongest card in the hand of the writer looking to generate new variations on old themes. The Joker, for example, has an origin as thoroughly worked out as any superhero: it was first set out in the story 'The Man behind the Red Hood' from *Detective Comics* 168 (1951). This story also forms the basis for a good deal of the plot of the 1989 Batman movie, and the material is also retold in Alan Moore and Brian Bolland's Batman story 'The Killing Joke' (1988). Originally wearing a red hood with no apparent eyeholes as a disguise for committing crimes, the Red Hood's features are disfigured in an escape through tanks of chemical waste at the Monarch Playing

Card Company's factory.

> That chemical vapour – it turned my hair green, my lips rouge red; my skin chalk white! I look like an evil clown! What a joke on me! Then I realized my new face could terrify people! And because the playing card company made my new face I named myself after the card with the face of a clown . . . The Joker![28]

The transformation is not a question of gaining powers, but of growing to fit a particular mask or costume – entering perfectly a role within the system of signs which constitute super-heroical myth. The Joker submits to the mythic role which misfortune casts on him, whilst Batman constructs a persona as a result of deliberate choice – a very non-Manichean view of good and evil. Barthes observed a similar process at work in his essay 'The World of Wrestling'.

> What is portrayed by wrestling is therefore an ideal understanding of things; it is the euphoria of men raised for a while above the constitutive ambiguity of everyday situations and placed before the panoramic view of a univocal Nature, in which signs at last correspond to causes, without obstacle, without evasion, without contradiction.[29]

Such an 'ideal understanding' is offered through the emblems of costume – both for heroes and villains – and the structure of continuity. It is this play of established signs around the narrative which provides much of the pleasure in reading the traditional superhero comic. Plots allow for the free expression of these signs, which divulge a system of meaning which is independent of the development of any particular story-line.

From time to time it is asserted that the plots of superhero comics are dull and formulaic. The initial plot development predictably leads to a violent confrontation with a costumed villain. A five page fight scene is the obligatory result. In a sense this is all perfectly true: superhero stories have not usually been based on the conventions of mystery or suspense, which are arguably the literary conventions which the unprepared reader takes to their reading of the comic. To avoid melodrama, narrative demands a unity of character and plot, or that character development should be the result of plot development. Characters treated in such a manner are 'rounded', they 'live', they are defined for us by 'decisions under pressure'. All this is true of the superhero, but much of it takes place through the development of the character's origin and powers over a protracted period of time, and generally as a result of internal conflicts rather than conflicts with villains. Supervillains are the engines of diachronic continuity. Heroes are generally obliged to defeat at least one supervillain per issue, but the events which lead up to the confrontation are normally initiated by the supervillain. The hero is in this sense passive: he is not called upon to act unless the status quo is threatened by the villain's plans.

As one might expect, plot structure has proliferated about this basic unit. Numerous approaches have been developed for handling the villain's role as protagonist. The villain's motivation may be greed (the Kingpin, Lex Luthor), political fanaticism (the Red Skull), a mania for power (Doctor Doom), social engineering (the original Magneto), psychotic revenge against society for sundry personal reasons (Bullseye, the Joker), or even metaphysical evil which presumes a Manichean view of universal order (Mr Mxyzptlk, Loki, Mephisto). The common outcome, as far as the structure of the plot is concerned, is that the villains are concerned with change and the heroes with the maintenance of the status quo. At the conclusion of the Alan Moore/Curt Swan two-part story 'Whatever Happened to the Man of Tomorrow?', the reader is let into the secret that Lois Lane's husband Jordan Elliott is the retired Superman. Nor is he Clark Kent – Jordan Elliott is a much more relaxed and confident individual. Jordan Elliott itself is a pun on Superman's father's name, Jor El. Jordan and Lois are living in blissful suburban anonymity:

> You really love it, don't you? Just going to work every day, taking out the garbage, changing Jonathan's diapers . . . all this normal stuff.
>
> Yup. Can't beat it . . . although maybe I could live without the diapers.[30]

The superhero at rest may be nursing no unacted desires, and needs only to be summoned like a genie from a bottle in order to redress all moral imbalances. This basic strategy of superhero plotting has created a severe problem for screenwriters engaged in transferring superhero material to the movie screen. The dilemma has been evaded in diverse ways; the first Superman film used for its 'first act' the origin material, in which the infant Superman is the protagonist of his own emergent myth. Subsequently the role of protagonist falls on the villainous Lex Luthor in the main plot, whilst Clark Kent/Superman remains as protagonist of the sub-plot, the love interest with Lois Lane. *Superman II* makes Superman into the protagonist by removing his superpowers, and pitting him against three superpowered beings from the Phantom Zone. The Batman movie employs Jack Nicholson's Joker to drive the plot for the whole of the film.

Superheroes are not called upon to act as the protagonists of individual plots. They function essentially as antagonists, foils for the true star of each story, the villain. Writers and artists recognize this fact (publishers even more so) by protecting their best villains jealously from poor handling or over-use. The superheroes are the protagonists of the myth which is constructed as an intertextual reading of their careers. Thus Batman is the protagonist of the Batman myth, the story of the young Bruce Wayne who saw his parents killed in front of his eyes and so spends the rest of his life warring on crime. Daredevil is the protagonist of the Daredevil myth: the academically gifted son of a broken-down boxer who trains secretly and acquires a strange radar sense when blinded in an accident. These myths are everywhere touched on and excited by the individual stories. Sometimes – satisfyingly for the reader – the shape of the individual story reflects back the form of the superhero's own myth.

3 Deciphering The Myths

Explicit Mythology: Thor

Just as other genres of comics have appropriated existing narrative mythologies (the Wild West, anthropomorphism, horror) so Siegel and Shuster created Superman from material already to hand: the myths of Samson, Hercules and so on. There has arguably been a tendency for comic creators to legitimize their offspring by stressing their resemblance to legendary heroes or gods: a strategy to give their disregarded medium a degree of moral and intellectual uplift. Billy Batson's cry of 'Shazam' that changed him into Captain Marvel is an acronym based on the initial letters of Solomon (for wisdom), Hercules (for strength), Atlas (for stamina), Zeus (for power), Achilles (for courage) and Mercury (for quickness). If the cry of 'Shazam' invokes anything, it's the collective prestige of the Roman and Greek pantheons. C.C. Beck's Captain Marvel stories liked to dabble with classical or Egyptian mythology, albeit in a throw away, tongue-in-cheek style. The *Captain Marvel* 100 story 'Captain Marvel battles the Plot Against the Universe'[1] is a fine example of the light-hearted use of explicit myths. The manner in which such 'high culture' elements are introduced into the story prefigures the way in which Marvel Comics – and in particular Stan Lee and Roy Thomas – were to make use of such elements in their superhero stories of the 1960s and 1970s.

The attitude towards knowledge in the superhero comic has always been a reverential one. Superman, Batman, and other heroes of the Golden Age tended to deal in scientific knowledge. Page 1 of *Action Comics* 1 begins with a brief explanation of Superman's amazing strength – in the style of information snippets from teenage magazines, or the later 'true comics' such as *Marvels of Science* and *Future World*. 'You may think the powers of Superman are incredible – but think! Science is discovering incredible new facts every week. Nothing is impossible in the long run.'[2] This might stand as an epigraph for the whole superhero genre. Science is used as an alibi for magic. Superman's vulnerability to green kryptonite is matched by his vulnerability to magic. As forces they are carefully distinguished, as if to demonstrate that kryptonite, by affecting Superman in a different way, is not magical and must therefore be scientific in its operation. A clear pair of structural opposites is built up within the mythology of the comic: what is not magical must be scientific – as noted in Chapter One. But as the operation of magic and unexplained science – such as green kryptonite – is indistinguishable, then what this bogus science/magic opposition really defines is Superman's overarching heroism, and his ability to make all systems of philosophy and science refer back to his own prepotent strength. Superman cannot be harmed by any force we recognize as part of our own universe – only by magic or magic masquerading as science. Superman's periodic humbling by either of these forces doesn't predispose the reader to imagine the hero vulnerable in any wider sense.

Many of us make use of the products of our technological civilization without understanding how they operate. Superhero comics offer this kind of 'scientific magic' at every turn – rockets, robots, mutants – but they are also adept at offering a more traditional kind of magic based on myth and religion. In particular, Lee and later Thomas hit on this vein with the creation of the Mighty Thor as a comic book character in 1962.

Thor has proved to be one of the most unusual creations in the history of comics: the first successful attempt to harness existing mythology on a large scale to construct the *mise en scène* of a superhero. Initially, Thor's alter ego Dr Donald Blake was portrayed as a man who came into the possession of a walking stick which could transform him into the Thunder God Thor. But, as the background of the comic was developed, Lee turned it all around and revealed that Dr Blake had been the Mighty Thor in disguise all the time, having been put into the body of a lame, earthbound doctor by his father Odin as a punishment for his arrogance in Asgard.

The popularity of Thor has not been duplicated by other superheroes based on traditional or legendary characters. Over-learned or overtly educational comics have failed often enough since the 1940s. Why was *The Mighty Thor* such a success? Some of the reasons might be these:

1. Jack Kirby's original artwork for the title rendered Thor, the supporting cast, Asgard and its inhabitants, the rainbow bridge Bifrost and all the villains and monsters in an accessible, science fiction/fantasy style that linked them comfortably with the rest of the Marvel Universe. Thor was a little bit different, admittedly, but the title fitted in all the same. Asgard might be the Norse heaven, but it was made approachable in the same way as an alien planet: strange, exotic, breath-taking, but not completely uncanny.[3] Kirby's rendition of Thor himself made the character's feats of strength and their context happily credible. Thor's costume, half traditional, half super-heroical, also stressed his participation in superhero continuity while emphasizing his somewhat privileged position within it. He stood clearly at the top of Marvel's pecking order: a match for Superman, should it ever become possible for them to meet in battle.

***Thor* 158, page 5. Jack Kirby's Dr. Black and Thor. *The Mighty Thor* 158, © Marvel Entertainment Group, Inc. 1968.**

***Thor* 158. Science meets magic in Kirby's Asgard. *The Mighty Thor* 158, © Marvel Entertainment Group, Inc. 1968.**

2. The expectations set up by the existing tissue of superhero mythologies. By 1962, there had already been 24 years of consecutive Superman publication, 23 of Batman, 19 of Wonder Woman. The mythologies of these and other characters were already established and complex. Suddenly it seemed possible to graft the whole of Norse mythology on to the Marvel Universe.

3. Thor is not an especially familiar character in contemporary Western culture. (Marvel comics have made him, and the whole Norse pantheon, intelligible to a whole new audience.) But the Norse gods are not alien either. Days of the week are named for them. Much of the pleasure in reading Thor comics is bound up with this reappropriation of a mythology so inconspicuously buried in the vocabulary of the reader's everyday speech.

4. Confidence: Lee and Thomas knew the effects they were aiming for. They saw the Asgardian characters as superheroes from a ready-made, legendary background – not as an excuse for reanimating the Eddas for a teenage audience. Ultimately Thomas was to go on to write Thor stories taken directly from the *Elder Edda* (such as *Thor* 272),[4] but only after a decade and a half of material had rounded out the character of the protagonist as conceived in the pages of the comic.

If Asgard could be fitted so neatly into the format of the superhero comic, it may be partly due to the fact that, since the advent of *Superman*, writers and artists had been working with such models consciously or half-consciously in mind. Without engaging in any exhaustive structural comparisons, it should be clear that the major pantheons of gods have certain features in common. The gods need somewhere to live – Asgard or Olympus – which is both remote and yet conveniently at hand, and comprehensible as a superlative form of the castles and palaces inhabited by earthly kings and queens. Odin's palace in Asgard, Valhalla, may have 540 doors, each wide enough to admit 800 men marching abreast, but it is still the palace of a warrior king: an astonishing structure built from familiar materials. None of this is wholly different from – say – the Fantastic Four's Baxter Building headquarters, or Wayne Mansion.

The gods also express a hierarchy contiguous with the demands of continuity – from Odin and Thor and Sif and Balder to the lesser gods Fandral, Hogun and the Vanir. The animist function of Norse mythology was intended to make the world more intelligible and more welcoming. But Norse mythology also embodies a characteristic which unites the extant Indo-European mythologies: the tripartite division of the pantheon into those connected with the government of the world, those connected with force and physical strength, and those connected with peace, pleasure and fecundity. Furthermore:

> Among the Germanic peoples, the Indo-European inheritance is represented by Woden [Odin] and Tiw in the first position, Donar [Thor] in the second, and the Vanir in the third. The representation of the first function by two divinities is a feature which the Teutons share with the Indian peoples . . . firstly, there is the ruler who is the priest king, who works by the incalculable and terrifying means of magic, and secondly, the king who reflects the order of the world and of society, the constitutional monarch, as it were, who incarnates law.[5]

Lee and Kirby's Thor does not literally reproduce this split between priest-king Odin and constitutional king Tiw, as Tiw is not included in the Marvel Universe's version of Asgard. Yet the underlying spirit of the mythology is preserved through the portrayal of Odin, who is seen sometimes as a benevolent, kindly king, and at others to be jealous, short tempered and unpredictable. This opposition is in many ways analagous to the social structure of many superhero comics, where authority and force are rigidly separated: as in the relationships existing between Commissioner Gordon and Batman, Professor Xavier and the original X-Men, or embodied within such split personalities as Matt Murdock/Daredevil and Jim Corrigan/The Spectre.

In recreating Thor for a 1960s readership, Lee and Kirby made several decisions about Norse mythology and its interpretation which may be signposts to Thor's popularity and durability as a comic-book hero. Thor's locus of action is New York, where most of the other Marvel superheroes live and operate, and where Thor can benefit from the vertical structure of the Manhattan skyline, swooping dramatically between skyscrapers in the style of Superman, Iron Man, or any of the other great airborne heroes. Secondly, Lee and Thomas were never reluctant to develop the humorous and even low-life side of Thor's character, which derives authentically from the Eddas. Thor is capable of being hoodwinked and outwitted, a quality which the Marvel Thor manages on some occasions to retain. But no one is more steadfast and loyal when the time comes for battle.

These attributes have often been most successfully developed in Thor's appearances as part of Marvel's all-star superhero team The Avengers. Thor is one of the founding members – along with Iron Man, The Wasp, Henry Pym (aka Ant-Man, Yellowjacket etc), and (very briefly in the beginning) the Incredible Hulk. Mixing with other key members of The Avengers such as Captain America, The Vision, the Scarlet Witch and Hawkeye, Thor evolved an earth-bound warrior persona which is both droll in its appeal and very much in accord with the impulsive and slightly gullible Thor of Teutonic myth.[6] Thor enjoys battling alongside comrades such as

***Avengers* 149, page 31. Thor explains the slow decline in his fighting ability. *The Avengers* 149, © Marvel Entertainment Group, Inc. 1976.**

Iron Man, Captain America and Hawkeye, even though he knows them to be vastly inferior to himself in raw power. He admires their heroism, and clearly enjoys his fellowship with them as much (if not more) than the more rarefied atmosphere of Asgard, where Odin frequently rebukes his adopted son for spending too much time on the concerns of 'that miserable mudball Midgard'.

After defeating Orka the human killer whale in *Avengers* 149, Captain America asks Thor why he was unable to defeat the monster until he unleashed his final, knockout punch. Thor's reply is typical of the witty and innovative *Avengers* scripts of Steve Englehart:

> The reason I did fail, Captain America, is that I be the God of Thunder. I am not slow-witted, but my task in the All-Father's plan doth concern itself more with action than reflection. What I saw not till this battle is that, to adapt myself to ye mortals I have accustomed myself to withold my full might.
>
> 'Twas a gradual thing. In Asgard, I have struggled against Gods. On Midgard, we have mostly met human menaces. To avoid the murder of these men – and to avoid the humbling of my friends – I came to act as less than I am. To thrill to the thunder of battle, I forgot I am the God thereof.[7]

This is almost a parable of Thor's induction into Marvel continuity: from God to comic-book superhero. The character has been fairly ruthlessly cut on the Procrustean bed of the superhero comic – and rarely used as a pretext for expounding Norse mythology. In this sense, the process of Thor's elevation to superhero is only a more explicit rendering of the process by which Siegel and Shuster conflated their knowledge of the myths of Samson, Hercules and the rest into the incarnation of Superman. *Thor* has successfully worn its high-culture credentials on its sleeve.

'Atonement with the Father': Superman

> For the son who has grown to really know the father, the agonies of the ordeal are readily borne; the world is no longer a vale of tears but a bliss-yielding, perpetual manifestation of the Presence.
>
> Joseph Campbell[8]

Very few superheroes have simple, uncomplicated relationships with their parents – especially those heroes who have 'come out' and abandoned (or never instigated) a secret identity. Some are old enough when they become superheroes to make a relationship with parental figures unnecessary – Mr Fantastic or Tony Stark, for example – but these characters tend to become involved in parental relationships from the position of the father. Reed Richards (Mr Fantastic) is husband (to the Invisible Woman) and a surrogate father-figure to the other members of the Fanstastic Four. Tony Stark acts as beneficiary to the Avengers superhero team as well as boss of a multinational corporation.

But Richards and Stark are relatively unusual: their superhero careers began at a time when they were already grown men, with established positions in society. More commonly, the roots of a superhero career – the all-important 'origin story' – go back to adolescence, and the character's development as a superhero must encompass evolving relationships with parents or substitute parental figures. The most satisfying and enduring superheroes have incorporated the familiar emotional landscape of adolescence into their developing superhero mythology. Their exploits very frequently dramatize the Oedipal conflict, or what Campbell refers to as the 'Atonement with the Father'.

This conflict is especially acute for the superhero. He will generally be the possessor of extraordinary physical and often mental powers, yet be unsure of his maturity and trustworthiness to use them. In any straight show-down with his father – in any trial of strength – he would clearly be triumphant. But such simplicity would be impermissible and unsatisfying as story or myth – it is never allowed to happen. Approval by the father is witheld time and again by the absence or unavailability of the father-figure.

Like Hercules, Superman appeared after a collision between the Earth and the Sky. His spaceship – sent to earth by his father Jor-El – strikes the Earth and leaves a deep scar to mark its arrival. (The depth of the furrow left by the infant Superman's spacecraft is clearly recognized as being important, and occurs in almost every portrayal of this key scene. In the Superman movie it is particularly deep, and the implicit phallus/vagina symbolism is hard to ignore).

Transplanted to earth, Superman's father is merely a memory kept fresh in the Fortress of Solitude – the retreat which Superman retires to for contemplation in the wastes of the Arctic circle. It's a suitably stern environment for the serious instruction in duty with which it is associated. Superman never rebels against his father's wisdom or authority in sending him to Earth – a role which he was given no chance to accept or decline. The father he does rebel against, however, is his earthly father, Mr Kent senior – leaving him behind to go to the city and make good at the earliest opportunity. Viewing Superman as the son of Jor-El leads one to conclude that he is a dutiful son with no trace of Oedipal conflict, happy to undertake the severe tasks imposed on him by his absent father. However, inverting the myth to give an oppositional reading where Clark Kent really is a boy made good from Smallville, we catch sight of an adolescent conflict noted by Freud in the essay 'Family Romances'.

> Small events in the child's life which make him feel dissatisfied afford him provocation for beginning to criticize his parents, and for using, in order to support his critical attitude, the knowledge which he has acquired that other parents are in some respects preferable to them . . . the child's imagination becomes engaged in the task of getting free from the parents of whom he now has a low opinion and of replacing them by others, who, as a rule, are of higher social standing.[9]

Most of us are kids from Smallville with parents who may not be as limited as the Kents, but might be able to support some improvement. And many might like to believe themselves the last survivor of a superhuman civilization, sent to Earth to be a saviour of humanity.

In fact, the Superman myth is such a resonant one that it can comfortably support a whole battery of contradictory interpretations, of which the Freudian/Oedipal element is only a single strand. Gary Engle proposes a reading of the myth in *Superman at Fifty*[10] which cites the Man of Steel as a superlative example of the successful immigrant – the orphan boy from the old country who makes it on his own in America. There seems to be no need to choose between such interpretations, when the myth is happily able to support both of them.

Alan Moore's two Superman stories – 'For the Man Who Has Everything' and 'Whatever Happened to the Man of Tomorrow?'[11] develop the character's relationship with the father figure a little further. In the former story, Superman experiences in an induced hallucination the way events would have shaped on Krypton, had the planetary destruction which caused his journey to Earth never taken place. Superman's father, Jor-El, is portrayed as a reactionary fanatic, bitterly clinging to the past, and almost regretful that the end of Krypton has failed to come to pass – as he predicted it would 20 years earlier:

> Look around you, Kal. What's happened to Krypton? There's the drug traffic in glamor-salts and hellblossom coming in from Erkol . . . there's racial trouble with the Vathlo island immigrants . . .
>
> Father, Krypton is changing. Extremist political groups aren't making it any easier . . .[12]

In 'Whatever Happened to the Man of Tomorrow?' Superman finally achieves the twin ambitions of marrying Lois Lane and retiring from the burden of being Superman. Restored to normal limitations, fatherhood beckons – Moore leaves us with a sight of the happily married couple drifting into middle age, washing diapers and munching takeaway pizzas in front of the TV set '... and after that, if Jonathan's quiet, I thought maybe bed with a bottle of wine.' Superman has finally grown up and become a father-figure himself (and likes it). But this story has been carefully labelled 'imaginary', and doesn't form any part of DC continuity.

A story which is part of the Superman continuity is the John Byrne/Karl Kesel collaboration in *Superman* 11 (1987), 'The Name Game'. Mr Mxyzptlk, a villain from the fifth dimension of almost omnipotent capabilities, drops by the offices of the *Daily Planet* one morning, in the guise of a macho character named Delroy, who is dressed to look more at home in an episode of *Miami Vice*. He mesmerizes Lois Lane with his chat-up lines, and invites her for a lunch date, to the consternation of Clark Kent. 'Lois . . . You have a lunch date today. With me!' Mxyzptlk eventually tires of Lois's company, and swaps her for a shop-window mannequin which he brings to life with nothing more than a gesture.

Clark, now transformed into Superman, discovers what's happened to Lois, but sees that, although apparently a mannequin, she is in fact still warm and alive. He follows the trail of destruction left by Delroy – but Delroy isn't sorry to be tracked down. 'Ah! Finally!! The very man I've been waiting for.' He destroys the woman-mannequin with another gesture, and then transforms himself from the *Miami Vice* look to the familiar comical-diabolical shape of Mr Mxyzptlk. 'Who are you?' asks Superman (it's the first time they've met since the relaunch of Superman's continuity in 1986). 'My real name would never translate into your clumsy Earth languages. All you need to know is that I am from a parallel dimension.'[13] Mxyzptlk demonstrates his absolute power over Superman by putting him through a disturbing series of physical transformations, before sportingly agreeing to a contest. 'I'll challenge you to the name game. All you have to do is get me to write, spell, or say my name backwards.' Mxyzptlk types out his untranslatable name on a giant typewriter created from a billboard illustration as easily as the mannequin was brought to life.

Some gratuitous but very satisfying destruction follows, as Mxyzptlk transforms the *Daily Planet* building into a walking colossus with the personality of a small child. Superman challenges Mxyzptlk to repeat his invented name by hitting the same keys as before on the giant typewriter. Mxyzptlk accepts the challenge, not realizing that Superman has rewired the machine to spell out the letters in reverse: Kltpzyxm. Mxyzptlk vanishes, threatening to return. His various acts of destruction are neutralized as he vanishes: next time we meet Lois she is earnestly discussing the

DC
DROP DEAD,
SUPERMAN
11
75¢
APPROVED BY THE COMICS CODE AUTHORITY
BY JOHN BYRNE & KARL KESEL
MISTER MXYZPTLK IS THE ONLY MAN FOR ME!
MILLENNIUM IS COMING
STEPPING INTO THE 5TH DIMENSION!

psychological effects of Mxyzptlk's visit on innocent bystanders.

This particular story carries a flavour of Superman stories from the 1950s and 1960s, although it plays self-consciously with the conventions it employs and undercuts itself with a strong vein of self-parody. But underneath the droll and witty trappings it's possible to detect another reworking of the Oedipus theme, with the supervillain standing in for the absent father-figure. A large and domineering male character appears who effortlessly steals Clark Kent's girlfriend. Superman gives chase. Superman discovers the intruder to be an all-powerful being whom Superman cannot hope to defeat in head-to-head combat. At the same time, his enemy is revealed as being a comical old man. Superman defeats the old man's menace by solving a riddle – and it is amusing and perhaps not wholly irrelevant to recall Oedipus and the riddle of the Sphinx. In the final showdown, Superman needs to resort to a stratagem which proves more effective than all his superhuman strength. The riddle solved, the menace is dissipated. Together with the 'extra effort' mentioned in chapter two, this is a common motif of superhero/supervillain conflict: the victory which is obtained all at one moment, through a mystical or intellectual key which unlocks the door to victory. It's relatively rare for Superman or any other high-powered superhero to achieve a victory by repeatedly bludgeoning his enemy into the ground. 'Extra effort' or 'riddle' victories are far more common.

If they were not, then Superman's most Oedipal foe of all, Lex Luthor, would scarcely stand a chance against the Man of Steel. Luthor has no special powers apart from his phenomenal scientific intelligence and his ruthless desire to exploit any stratagem, no matter how immoral, if its prosecution might lead to Superman's destruction. In his essay 'The Good, The Bad and The Oedipal', Lester Roebuck lists the ways in which Luthor resembles an evil version of Superman's father, Jor-El. Both are scientific geniuses of the highest order – but Luthor uses his power to attempt world domination, while Jor-El uses his to try to save Krypton. In *Superman* 70 (1964) Luthor manages to travel back in time to Krypton before Jor-El's marriage to Superman's mother: he plans to woo her away from Jor-El, marry her and thus eliminate the menace of Superman before he is even born. Roebuck suggests that this episode is doubly Oedipal:

> Not only does it underscore the role Luthor plays as the symbolic evil

'Drop Dead, Superman, Mister Mxyzptlk is the only man for me!'. Oedipal trouble in *Superman* 11, 1987.

> father, it introduces the other half of the Oedipal myth as well. Luthor – the evil alter ego with whom Superman is inextricably bound – dares to enter into a sexual relationship with the Super Mother.[14]

Superman has often been curtly dismissed as an adolescent fantasy of omnipotence. On closer inspection, a diametrically opposed reading emerges: Superman is all about powerlessness. Time and again, Superman's great physical powers are useless when set against the trickery, deceit and immorality of his enemies – most of all, Luthor. Again, this touches on the theme of atonement with the father; the growing teenage boy discovers that, despite his increasingly adult appearance, he is still legally and morally a child in the eyes of his parents. Very often (as in the Mxyzptlk story above) there is some kind of riddle to be solved before the world can be set in order again, and the hostile father-figure put in its place.

Superman's celibacy should also be taken into account, a quality he shares with popular heroes in line of descent from Sir Galahad to Agent Cooper in *Twin Peaks*. Virginity and celibacy have often been held to confer exceptional strength on the male warrior, as Sir James Frazer notes in *The Golden Bough*:

> Not only the warrior in the field but his friends at home will often bridle their sensual appetites from a belief that by so doing they will the more easily overcome their enemies.[15]

The celibacy myth is completed when we discover (in both the movie *Superman II* and the Moore/Swan collaboration 'Whatever happened to the man of Tomorrow') that in order to marry Lois Lane, Superman must give up his physical strength and invulnerability. To enter the adult world, the fantasy life must be left behind. Superman is an Oedipal myth for the century which invented the liminal states of teenager and adolescent, when physical mastery of the world precedes social mastery. Superman is adolescence writ large.

'Angry All Your Life': Batman

Like Superman, both Batman's parents are dead. But unlike Superman, Batman knew them as a child, witnessing their deaths at the hands of a minor-league hit man named Joe Chill. Chill was later discovered by Batman to have been part of a more far-reaching conspiracy against his father, who had managed to make dangerous enemies in the criminal fraternity. Shocked by the brutal murder of his parents, the young Bruce Wayne swore to wage war on crime and, in particular, the use of firearms, 'the coward's weapon'. He chooses the bat costume and identity to prey on the criminal's sense of guilt. In the famous words from *Batman* 47; 'Criminals are a superstitious, cowardly lot, so I must wear a disguise that will strike terror into their hearts! I must be a creature of the night, like a . . . a . . . A Bat!'

Most readers agree that Batman's origin is the most satisfying of all the major superheroes. The motif of vigilante revenge and street violence has made the character adaptable (one might be tempted to say almost too easily adaptable) to some of the social concerns of recent years. It explains his war on crime, his melancholy, his protectiveness towards Robin, and the ruthlessness of his methods. Every Batman story is to some extent an extension of the origin story, as Batman's motivation is wholly derived from the trauma of witnessing his parents shot in cold blood. But – clearly – no amount of successful crimefighting can ever undo his parents' death or alleviate the guilt to which Wayne is perpetually subjected. Two celebrated stories, 'The Origin of the Batman' (1948) and 'The First Batman' (1956), track down Joe Chill, the gunman responsible for his parents' death, and ultimately Lew Moxon, the gangland leader that Wayne Senior was investigating and who arranged for the murder.[16] The guilty men are brought to justice – but there is no question of Batman turning in his cape.

Sherlock Holmes took to detection as a protest against the monotony of existence. Batman takes the same course out of an obsessive need to expunge his sense of guilt and failure towards his parents. Indeed, this motivation is almost overly explicit and verges on being over-stated: brooding moments alongside the Waynes' gravestone run a risk of being weakened by over use.[17] A recent example is the opening of the Archie Goodwin/Dan Jurgens/Dick Giordano *Detective Comics Annual* 1990, opening with Batman standing in moonlight beside his parents' grave.

What makes Batman so different from Superman is that his character is formed by confronting a world which refuses to make sense. His experiences might have taught him to be wholly cynical – yet he continues to risk life and limb in a one-man war against crime. Most of his arch-enemies speak in riddles. The Penguin, The Joker, The Riddler, Two-Face, The Scarecrow, all in their own way suggest qualities which, whilst evil or antisocial in their results, derive from a radical inability to function in the everyday world – in short, sketches of various types of madness. All Batman's most effective scripters and artists have understood that this madness is a part of Batman's special identity, and that the protagonist's obsessive character links him with his enemies in a more personal way than, say, Superman.[18]

Arguably the key Batman villain is Two-Face – less familiar than others because he was never used on the 1960s' TV series. Two-Face was formerly Harvey Dent, District Attorney, who turned to a life of crime when half of his face was horrifically disfigured by acid. Two-Face regards himself as being equally divided between good and evil, and tosses a silver dollar defaced on one side to determine whether the good or evil side of his character should prevail in any decision. Two-Face unites both a Manichean philosophy (good and evil conveniently separated yet parts of a greater whole) and the random element (he makes decisions on the toss of a coin). Batman's skills as a detective are transmutative, producing order from chaos, solutions from mystery, justice from injustice, and even good from evil. His world, as much as any superhero's, is one of mirror images and opposites. Robin's chirpiness and brightly-coloured costume contrast purposefully with Batman's appearance and personality. Commissioner Gordon's concern for justice to the letter of the law mirrors Batman's justice which goes far beyond the law. Even the weighty formality of Alfred the butler – who really is what he seems – highlights a contrast with his employer Bruce Wayne, who is in reality so much more.

The great Batman villains all mirror some key point in Batman's character, a point of reference which gives their villainy special purchase within the metatext of the Batman myth. The Penguin provides a droll commentary on the easy assimilation of Batman's ascetic and asexual persona into the world of Gotham city: the Penguin shows the campy side of Bruce Wayne given free rein. The Joker epitomizes the dark and negative side of the personal obsessions which fuel Batman's crimefighting career: the Joker is a constant reminder that strength which derives from traumatic experience can be turned towards evil as easily as good. Two-Face redoubles the force of this assertion, the more so because his split personality (itself mirroring the Bruce Wayne/Batman duality) belongs to an individual who was once an officer of the law.

In *Detective Comics* 500 (1981), Batman finally gained the opportunity to avenge the deaths of his parents, in the Alan Brennert/Dick Giordano collaboration 'To Kill A Legend'. Haunted by dreams of his parents' death, Batman is approached by the mysterious interdimensional being known as the Phantom Stranger. The Stranger explains that on a trans-dimensional parallel earth another attempt on Bruce Wayne's parents' life is about to take place. The attempt will be a successful one unless Batman and Robin are sent to intervene. Batman is taken aback by the offer.

> Intervene? You mean – travel to this other earth and stop the murder. But – why are you offering me this?
>
> You are a brave man, Bruce Wayne . . . But despite all your courage,

> all the good you've done . . . you still feel you failed the ones you loved the most.[19]

On arrival, the parallel earth turns out to be different to Batman's in certain important ways – as Robin observes:

> What a strange world! Plenty of crime, terrorism, war – but not a single costumed hero! Of course, there weren't any costumed heroes on our own earth till a few decades ago – but – there doesn't seem to be any heroic mythology on this earth either! No Robin Hood – No Camelot – No Hercules, Odysseus, Gilgamesh – Even that wouldn't bother me, though, if it weren't for this! According to this star atlas, the red star around which Krypton is supposed to orbit doesn't exist! If there's no Krypton in this dimension, then they'll be no Superman – perhaps no super-powered heroes at all! And with no literature to inspire them – this might be a world without heroes – except for its Batman.
>
> That's supposition, Dick – not deduction.[20]

This is intertextuality of a fairly high order. Batman's 'parallel world' is initially likened to our own – plenty of crime, but no costumed heroes. The reader feels for a moment the potency that the Batman myth might have if the character really existed. But the text distances us again by explaining that familiar legends such as Robin Hood and Odysseus are as unknown on this earth as costumed superheroes. Superman is carefully introduced into the discourse, as a final term in the list beginning Hercules, Odysseus, Gilgamesh . . .

Clearly, this part of the story sets up the significance of Batman's decision to save his parents' life. In so doing, he may be denying this earth the one chance it has to gain a hero worthy of the name. The text plays with different levels of fiction and reality (and in so doing strengthens the mythological 'weight' of Batman and Superman by bracketing them with Robin Hood and Odysseus). Such intertextual juggling demands that the reader come to some hierarchical positioning of Batman and Superman within a pantheon of heroes wider than the whole of DC's continuity. We continue reading with a renewed sense of Batman's significance as a legend, both to his world and our own.

Batman and Robin stand guard over the Wayne family, observing that the young Bruce Wayne displays all the characteristics of a spoiled brat: not a likely candidate to grow up into a superhero. Batman is tormented by the sight of his dead parents seemingly restored to life. Eventually, when the murderous attack comes – in an unexpected way – Batman and Robin are able to thwart the killer. The Phantom Stranger instantly transports them back to their own dimension. Robin wants to know more:

Will we ever know what'll happen – to young Bruce, his life?

Perhaps. But for now, all you need to know is that you saved two lives . . . and altered forever a third.[21]

'Amen to that' echoes Batman. But an epilogue to the story shows the young Bruce Wayne of the parallel earth going through some changes. Gone is the spoiled brat who threw his model trains at his mother. The young boy is already turning into the Bruce Wayne who'll grow up to be Batman: working out, reading Sherlock Holmes (one hero which this parallel world does seem to have), and reading up on the psychology of crime.

That night Bruce Wayne learned what death was . . . and he learned it could be averted . . . at least temporarily. Years from now, he will make a decision . . . choose a direction for his life . . . and when he does, it will not be a decision born out of grief, or guilt, or vengeance . . . but of awe . . . and mystery . . . and gratitude.[22]

These words are laid over the story's final panel, which shows the young Wayne walking down the driveway of his parents' mansion, casting the shadow of the Batman before him.

Consistent with the story's theme of loops and repetitive events, the artwork produces a number of echoes that underscore these processes. Most notable is the deliberate system of parallels between Bruce Wayne's dream of the death of his parents on page 2, and the intervention of Batman and Robin to prevent the Waynes' death on the parallel Earth. Panel 3 of page 17 exactly repeats panel 1 of page 2, in everything but the slight differences in the attacker's clothing, and the more intense colouring – the second time is for real, while page 2 was only a dream. Moreover, the dialogue repeats word-for-word through these panels and into the following pair – panel 2 on page 2 and panel 4 on page 17:

What – What is this . . .?

It's called a stick-up, buddy! I'll take that necklace the lady's wearin'

You hoodlum! Don't you dare put your hand on my wife![23]

The artwork for panels 2–4, however, is a complete contrast. In the dream sequence we see Thomas Wayne reaching out to grasp Joe Chill and being shot down, while in the 'alternate earth' sequence the lines of dialogue are laid over a panel showing Robin about to leap into action. Chill's next words in the dream sequence are also in panel 2 and are addressed to Wayne senior – 'Maybe now you'll keep quiet', as he fires at point blank range into Wayne's chest.

Panel 5 of the alternate earth sequence has the line 'Maybe this'll shut you up' spoken as Batman interposes his body between the gun

Detective Comics **500, page 2.**

***Detective Comics* 500, page 17.**

and the Wayne family. On page 2, in the dream sequence, we see the firing of the gun at close range, as if from the point of view of young Bruce, witnessing his parents' murder. The third panel, a circular punctuation mark in the Kane tradition, shows the firing of the gun: 'CLICK!'. The dialogue 'An' this . . . will shut you up lady!' carries over into panel 4, which shows Chill's face from a menacing, low angle. The gun fires towards but not directly at the reader: young Bruce's view of his mother being shot while standing next to him. The explosive sound effect 'BLAM!' and the flame from the gun-barrel are a splash of red and yellow in an otherwise almost monochromatic sequence of panels.

Panel 5 of page 17 also shows Batman looking at the killer from a low angle, as he dives in to grab the attacker's arm from underneath. The effect of this acrobatic move, however, is momentarily to reduce Batman to the stature of a child as he prevents this second murder of his parents. The Wayne family stand terrified in the top left of the panel, while Batman's reaching arms strain beyond the panel's borders in his effort to prevent history repeating itself. Batman can barely be contained within the page, and neither can the attacker, whose hand and foot are literally forced out of the picture by the ferocity of Batman's attack.

Panel 5 of page 2 corresponds with the full-width panel 6 of page 17. Page 2 shows the young Bruce Wayne staring up from the panel's bottom left in helpless rage at the attacker:

> F-Father . . . Mother . . . They're dead! You killed them!
>
> S-Stop lookin' at me like that, kid! Stop lookin' at me![24]

Panel 6 of page 17 reverses this position, as Batman stares ferociously at the attacker – his rage clearly visible despite the mask he wears. The gun, held aloft and still smoking on page 2, falls from the fleeing attacker's grasp. On page 17 it is shown directly above the living group of the Wayne family, as it was smoking over the corpses of Mr and Mrs Wayne on page 2. The light source of both panels is a lamp-post in the centre rear. On page 2 the actual lamp is hidden – its light falls in ghostly rings over the scene of carnage and young Bruce's impotent rage. On page 17 we see the lamp directly casting its light over the unharmed Wayne family, shielding them from harm as much as the advancing figure of Batman.

'To Kill a Legend' was the lead-off piece in the giant-sized *Detective Comics* 500, an anniversary celebration of the title and its chief hero. Two other Batman stories were included, along with material featuring the Hawkman, the Elongated Man, plus Slam Bradley and a posse of other private eyes revived from the earliest, pre-Batman days of the title. The text risks the whole identity of the hero it will continue to inscribe, secure in the understanding that, in revealing the possibility of a wholly different Batman, it is fastening more securely to the Batman of DC continuity. This complication of the metatext points out the impossibility of Batman ever fully atoning for the death of his parents: 'No one should be angry all his life, Dick.' A Batman without anger is a Batman retired. Batman is never allowed to know that his actions on the alternative earth led to the creation of a new Bruce Wayne/Batman via a different psychological route. A complete atonement might spell retirement, which continuity can never permit.

'Living in the New Middle Ages'

Superhero narratives clearly give substance to certain ideological myths about the society they address: the USA. A narrative such as Thor confronts ideological myth-making very directly: it places the traditional hero or God on the stage of American society. Thor's heroism and integrity become a barometer by which can be measured the character of those he encounters. Other remarkable beings such as the Silver Surfer (an alien), Doctor Strange (Master of the Mystic Arts) or the Spectre (a ghost) function in the same way: apart from providing a magnificent set of heroic qualities, they also examine society through the window of their own very peculiar viewpoint. The odd thing about Superman is that he doesn't provide such an angle of view: culturally, Superman is completely American.

This strategy of viewing the world through the eyes of a remarkable outsider makes a very clear statement of how most superhero narratives view their host culture. Far from being as 'escapist' as is claimed, most superhero comics are intensely grounded in the normal and everyday. There is a constant delight in showing the mundane nature of daily life. In part, this is a strategy to build up suspense and contrast: a supervillain like Doctor Doom or Magneto can be made to seem so much more threatening against a background of recognizable reality. But there is another reason as well. Superheroes are by and large not upholders of the letter of the law; they are not law enforcement agents employed by the state. The set of values they traditionally defend is summed up by the Superman tag of 'Truth, Justice and the American Way'. Sometimes the last term has been interpreted in a narrowly nationalistic sense; superheroes have on occasions become uncritical supporters of US foreign policy. But far more often the third term has stood for the ideals enshrined in the US constitution. Superheroes have been better Americans – as the founding fathers would have understood the term – than most of America's modern political leaders.

Captain America – inescapably a patriotic icon – was forced to go through an agonizing readjustment of his political outlook in a series of Steve Englehart stories written in the aftermath of the Watergate scandal. Disgusted by corruption within government circles, he abandoned the Captain America identity to become plain Steve Rogers, then made a tentative superhero comeback as the Nomad – one who does not have a home. During this long-running storyline from 1974–75, Steve Rogers battled a couple of false Captain Americas who stepped in to fill his vacant shoes, and was encouraged to return to his Captain America identity by his black superhero partner The Falcon.

In *Captain America* 177 the Falcon tries unsuccessfully to persuade Steve Rogers not to throw in the towel. Getting a negative response, he vows from that moment on to go it alone:

> You taught me to play the super-hero game, so I'm gonna play it . . . and I'm not lookin' back! Goodbye and good luck!
>
> Sam! . . . Is this the way it's going to be now? Follow my conscience . . . and lose my friends . . . lose everything except my self-respect? Lord, I hope not![25]

At the word 'Sam!' The Falcon flies away, and Steve is left speaking the remaining words to himself. Cap's recovery of his full identity and costume is abetted by the Falcon's loyalty to a particular version of the American Dream. As embodied by Captain America, the American Dream equals self-improvement – Steve Rogers, once a skinny weakling, was transformed by the power of science into a super-soldier and patriotic symbol. The Englehart/Watergate stories involved turning the Captain America legend inward on itself – did post-Watergate, post-Vietnam America still deserve its heroes?

But the Captain America iconography can be used in contrasting ways. Take, for example, the cover of the Captain America special of 1990, 'Captain America goes to war against drugs.' The comic was produced in co-operation with the FBI, and contains on the inside cover a list of government departments which have reviewed its contents, as well as a list of 56 FBI offices which have a 'Drug Demand Reduction Coordinator'.

The story shows a young baseball player, Mitch, a star pitcher, who is offered cocaine by an alien space monster to help him relax before a game. Captain America solves Mitch's problems, mainly through providing moral support. The cover, however, doesn't show a scene from the story inside. Instead, it depicts an allegorical scene in which Captain America throws his red, white and blue shield at the word 'DRUGS', while a multi-ethnic, multi-gender group of teenage kids look on and cheer. The kids' clothes and

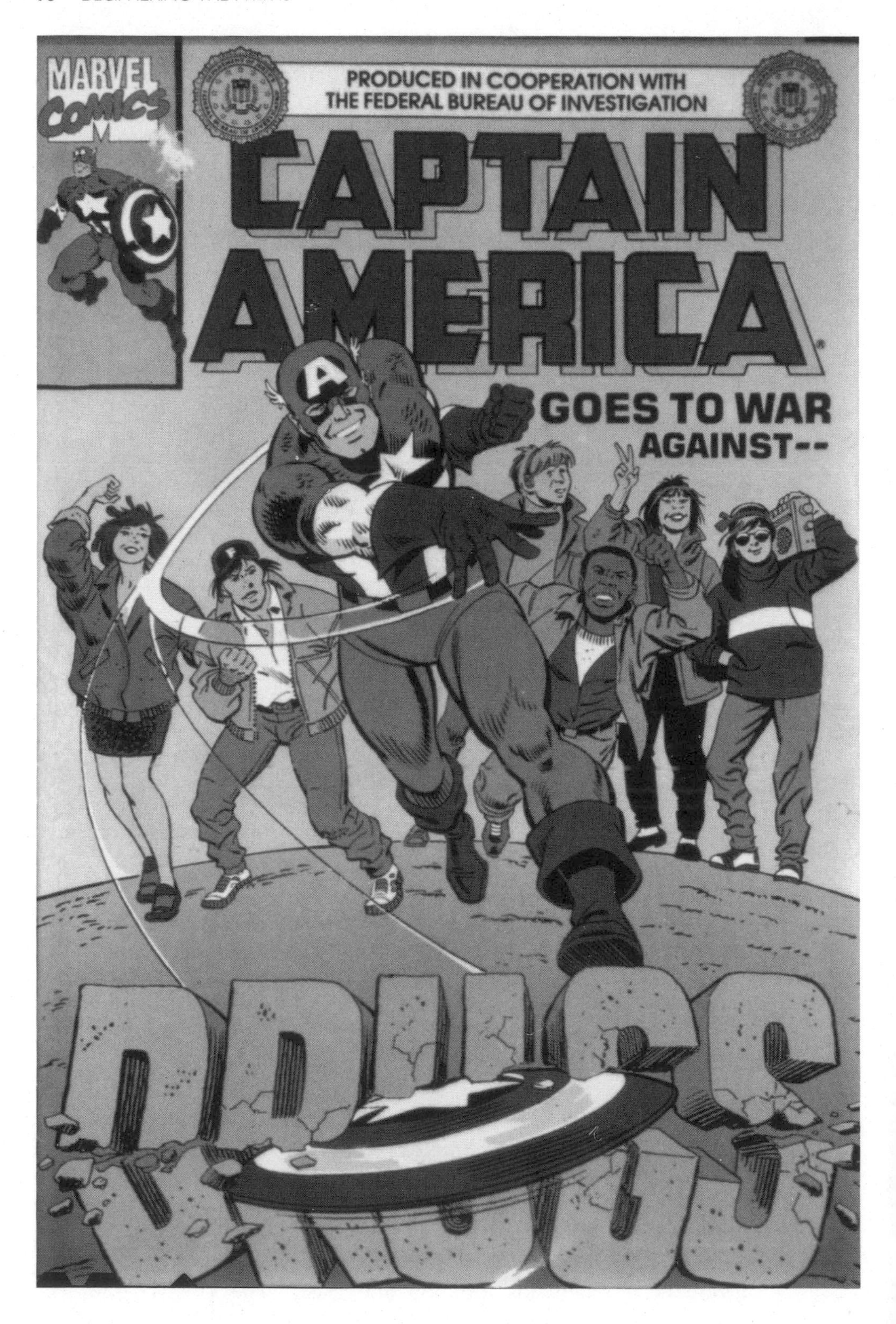

MARVEL COMICS
PRODUCED IN COOPERATION WITH THE FEDERAL BUREAU OF INVESTIGATION
CAPTAIN AMERICA
GOES TO WAR AGAINST--
DRUGS

accessories show them to be personifications of American urban youth – placed against a smooth, green background which is further universalized by the high angle of view.

The ideological strategy of this cover is to say: 'We're on the same side'. A comic-book narrative or cover design can effortlessly draw conflicting elements into a visual relationship, thus apparently resolving any contradictions which might have seemed to exist. There seems to be only the one way to decode this image: Captain America and American youth are on the same side, have the same agenda, are fighting for the same ideals.

Continuity, and the ability of sequential art to resolve contradictions simply by including them in the same panel, has made it difficult for black superheroes to inscribe any ideological values of their own. But it certainly couldn't be said that black superheroes haven't become numerically stronger as the years have gone by: The Black Panther, Power Man, The Falcon, Storm of the X-Men, Cyborg of the Teen Titans, and the black incarnations of Captain Marvel and the Punisher have all established themselves since the late sixties. Yet it is one thing to decree black superheroes, quite another to inscribe a plausible ideology for them.

A key ideological myth of the superhero comic is that the normal and everyday enshrines positive values that must be defended through heroic action – and defended over and over again almost without respite against an endless battery of menaces determined to remake the world for the benefit of aliens, mutants, criminals, or sub-aqua beings from Atlantis. The normal is valuable and is constantly under attack, which means that almost by definition the superhero is battling on behalf of the status quo. Into this heroic matrix one can insert representatives of any race or creed imaginable, but in order to be functioning superheroes they will need to conform to the ideological rules of the game. The superhero has a mission to preserve society, not to re-invent it.

The most effective form of social comment in superhero narratives is therefore satire. It has always been possible to use the satirical method from inside the political consensus or status quo in order to denounce the outstanding follies and abuses of the age – without suggesting or accepting that there is anything fundamentally wrong with the status quo's ideology. The Falcon became an effective vehicle for this kind of satire during his membership of The Avengers from *Avengers* 181 to 194. Drafted into the team against the wishes of some members (chiefly Hawkeye) as a quota represent-

***Captain America goes to war against drugs,* © Marvel Entertainment Group, Inc. 1976.**

"WONDER WOMAN? JEEZ--SHE'S A FOX! ONE BODACIOUS BOD, KNOWUDDAMEAN?? I'M REALLY INTO BIG, MUSCULAR BABES.
"YEAH, RIGHT, 'N' I LIKE THE WAY SHE MOVES, Y'KNOW, IN THAT METAL UNDERWEAR? HOTTER 'N PAULA ABDUL, EVEN."

"TO TELL YOU THE TRUTH, I THINK THE WHOLE THING'S GOTTEN A LITTLE OUT OF HAND.
"GOD, THAT WONDER WOMAN IS EVERY-WHERE!

"I'M GETTING KINDA TIRED SEEING MY HUSBAND OGLING HER PICTURES ALL THE TIME.
"I MEAN, SHE'S SO DROP-DEAD GORGEOUS, GOT ALL THESE GREAT POWERS, AND SHE'S A PRINCESS, FOR PETE'S SAKE. DOES SHE HAVE TO FLAUNT IT?"

"MY MAIN CONCERN IS THE EFFECT ALL THIS WONDER WOMAN HYSTERIA MAY BE HAVING ON OUR CHILDREN.
"WHAT DOES THAT GOLDEN WINGED DOUBLE-W REALLY MEAN?

"IS IT JUST SOME INNOCUOUS TRADEMARK, A STATUS SYMBOL, OR SOMETHING MORE INSIDIOUS-- A CULT SYMBOL REPRESENTING ALL SORTS OF PAGANISTIC NOTIONS?
"IS WONDER WOMAN PREACHING PEACE, OR JUST PREACHING? IF SHE IS SOME SORT OF RELIGIOUS APOSTLE, THEN SHE SHOULD SAY AS MUCH."

Ms.
AMAZONS
"I DUNNO. I JUST LIKE HER, Y'KNOW? I DON'T REALLY CARE ABOUT GODS AND STUFF. I JUST THINK SHE'S SO COOL!

"SHE CAME AND TALKED AT MY SCHOOL AND TOLD US HOW WE ALL HAD THIS POWER INSIDE US.
"THAT NO MATTER HOW BAD THINGS GOT, THE POWER WOULD GET YOU THROUGH IT ALL. WE JUST HAD TO BELIEVE IN IT."

"SHE LET ME TOUCH HER LASSO ONCE. WOW! IT FELT LIKE MY WHOLE BODY WAS FLOATING.
"ALL YOUR FEARS JUST SORT OF FLOAT AWAY FOR A WHILE. IT'S SO... PEACEFUL.

"THAT'S THE WAY DIANA MAKES YOU FEEL, LIKE SHE'S, Y'KNOW, A PART OF YOU.
"SHE'S EVERYBODY'S BEST FRIEND --BUT TO ME, SHE'S MORE LIKE A SISTER."

ing minorities, The Falcon was under pressure to prove himself to the rest of the team – despite support from his erstwhile partner Captain America. The Falcon finally comes good in a battle with the Grey Gargoyle (*Avengers* 190–191) but then quits the team three issues later;

> What I mean is that the main reason I joined the Avengers was to fill a government quota – and that quota no longer exists . . . so I'm handing in my walking papers. Maybe that'll ease some of the tension I seem to have brought in with me.

Captain America replies:

> I . . . don't think anyone really noticed, Falcon. But if you've made your decision, we'll honor it.[26]

The script by Dave Michelinie manages to satirize the situation pertaining to black superheroes: they are present in effect to fill up a quota, without offering anything different or unique which challenges the superhero status quo. Oppositional readings of certain comics may, however, throw up a different ideological perspective. For example, the whole theme of the X-Men – the isolation of mutants and their alienation from 'normal' society – can be read as a parable of the alienation of any minority. The original Magneto and his Brotherhood of Evil Mutants,[27] who disdained to cooperate with homo sapiens, could be read as an example of a minority grouping determined to force its own place within society. Such oppositional readings of the X-Men are possible – gay readings of the mutant subtext have been fairly common in the letter columns over the years.[28] But such exercises seem to be little more than efforts to wrench the subtext of the comic into a desired oppositional reading, rather than a fully engaged exploration of the open possibilities of the text – and of the nuances and subtleties which function as irony and satire, and therefore debunk or defang any absolutely oppositional reading.

This leads to the even more vexed subject of gender and of women superheroes. How can women who dress up in the styles of 1940s pornography be anything other than the pawns or tools of male fantasy? There has certainly been a sufficient quantity of powerful women superheroes – back to Wonder Woman in 1941, the Good Girl heroines of the late 1940s, the Batgirl and Supergirl offshoots, the various Marvel superheroines from the Scarlet Witch and the Black Widow to the She-Hulk and the new (black) Captain

***Wonder Woman* 49, page 9 (1990). Members of the public give a cross-section of views on America's number one superheroine.**

Marvel. But any feminist critic could demonstrate that most of these characters fail to inscribe any specifically female qualities: they behave in battle like male heroes with thin waists and silicone breasts, and in repose are either smugly domestic (the Invisible Woman, the Wasp) or brooding and remote – a slightly threatening male fantasy (Wonder Woman, or the Scarlet Witch).

It's easy to look at superhero comics and list the issues they fail to address. The relationship between the Vision and the Scarlet Witch, as it developed from *Avengers* 100 or so onwards, is a good example of how a mainstream Marvel title has mythologized the sex life of its characters over a considerable period of time. The Scarlet Witch, generally aloof in her manner, is an extremely powerful heroine, able to affect reality in unpredictable ways with her Hex power, which is a combination of magical and Mutant abilities (she was once a member of Magneto's Brotherhood of Evil Mutants, and is in fact Magneto's daughter). She has a voluptuous figure, shown off only too effectively by her red 'bathing costume' outfit and long trailing cloak. Cool in a crisis, her powers have many times saved the day against some of the Avengers' most formidable foes. The Vision likewise is a severe prospect for any supervillain. A synthetic android robot with an artificial 'human' personality, he has the ability to increase or reduce his body density to an unlimited extent. The Vision can become insubstantial or infinitely heavy and hard. He can also project destructive heat rays from his eyes, and has advanced computer-like intellectual faculties – a perfect example of the 'science as magic' motif discussed in chapter one. Over the years, these two became lovers, and eventually husband and wife. The Scarlet Witch's brother, himself the mutant superhero Quicksilver, has often shown disapproval of the marriage, disgusted that his sister should have wed a 'soulless machine'.[29]

There is clearly a pornographic subtext to this relationship, of the kind discussed in chapter two. But the Scarlet Witch's sexuality is presented blatantly the more firmly to deny it: no member of the Avengers has ever been known to remark on her revealing costume and sexy appearance. Such remarks just don't get made: the frisson of fetishistic sexuality is adduced with one hand only to be dismissed with the other. Sexuality is simultaneously presented – from the male point of view – in all its tempting erotic trappings – and then controlled, or domesticated, by a simple denial of its power and appeal.

Yet none of these adolescent contradictions might be seen to apply to a character like the Vision – cool, calculating and robot-like. If anyone can ignore or see past the Scarlet Witch's surface sexuality, it must be him: the 'soulless machine', who is immune to all temptations of the flesh. In fact, the robotic Vision is only a slightly more extreme version of the typical straight-laced superhero character, and his relationship with the Scarlet Witch an example of the reconciliation of opposites which is the stock-in-trade of the ideological subtext of many superhero comics. The mythology has moved on a little from the sado-masochism of William Moulton Marston's alluring woman a man is 'proud to submit to.' Instead, the myth could be described as an unearned state of post-feminism, and carries the message for both male and female readers: 'You can have your cake and eat it'. For women, the subtext might be read as 'You can dress sexy and still be taken seriously and hold a position of power'. For men: 'Just because you like her to wear sexy clothes doesn't mean you're degrading her status and equality.'[30] This is clearly a comfortable and comforting myth which can be found expressed rather differently in any issue of *Cosmopolitan*, *New Woman* or any of the other post-feminist women's magazines. Yet it could be argued that the superheroes arrive at this comfortable position via a slightly tougher route. The male superheroes embody a correspondingly exaggerated and kinky form of macho sex appeal, which puts them, in the fetish stakes, on a par with many of the superheroines.

As superhero comics have been and largely still are an art-form conceived with an adolescent audience at least partly in mind, it is wise to refer these issues of gender politics back to the viewpoint of an adolescent. It's also significant to bear in mind how deeply the Oedipus myth is embedded in the mythology of many of the key male superheroes. In their simultaneous offering and denying of sexuality, plus their cool strength and determination in battle with supervillains, the superheroines offer a reconciliation of all the conflicting demands of adolescent male sexual desire. Sexuality is domesticated (i.e. made safe) and yet remains exceptionally exciting. Women are visually thrilling, and yet threatening and dangerous only to outsiders and strangers.

The mythologizing of sexuality is a potential key to the ways in which superhero myths address the questions of power and justice within the societies they depict and/or reflect. Superheroes are always moving between extremes, and the greatest superhero artists excel at giving these contrasts a visible form. Murky film noir interiors cut to the wide open spaces above the rooftops; the splendour of New York from the air contrasts with the squalour at street level. Goodness and corruption co-exist. This must be so, because of the continuity of the stories: menaces can never be finally defeated, and the episodic, soap-opera plots support the notion that all victories are temporary.

After a serious menace has been cleared up, which may involve the termination of plots and subplots stretching back for a year or more, a subsequent issue will often begin with a deliberate 'clean slate' panel or panels. Often the 'clean slate' panel involves the superhero looking down at a birds-eye view of a calm and peaceful city. Such panels may occur on the last page of the issue concluding a plot-line, or the first page of the following installment. Either way, it seems for the moment that things are working out – evil has finally been brought under control. But a fully engaged reader knows it's only an illusion: new menaces will be popping up before long. The heroes need to triumph in the short term, but they can never be said to live happily ever after.

Society is constantly in transition, nothing will stay where you put it. This is an aspect of the superhero myth which has undergone considerable change over the lifetime of the genre. The comics of the 1940s and 1950s are set against a background of greater stability, and the heroes battled menaces which were either abnormally-motivated products of their society (The Joker, Lex Luthor), or else external menaces. Within the last 30 years, all this has changed. The normality which the superhero sees as so valuable seems to be constantly in a state of seige. The situation in superhero continuity is becoming an image of society as pictured by Umberto Eco in his essay 'Living in the new Middle Ages'.

Eco argues that contemporary society is coming to resemble or reconstruct the middle ages, and that the perceived breakdown of the Pax Americana is a modern equivalent to the collapse of the Roman Empire.

> What is required to make a good Middle Ages? First of all, a great peace that is breaking down, a great international power that has unified the world in language, customs, ideologies, religions, art, and technology, and then at a certain point, thanks to its ungovernable complexity, collapses. It collapses because the 'barbarians' are pressing at its borders; these barbarians are not necessarily uncultivated, but they are bringing new customs, new views of the world. These Barbarians may burst in with violence, because they want to seize a wealth that has been denied them, or they may steal into the social and cultural body of the reigning Pax, spreading new faiths and new perspectives of life.[31]

Eco is speaking of Western or global culture, but his remarks are intended to apply to the US itself, the instigator of the Pax Americana. Superhero comics had relatively little to do with the mythologizing of the Cold War,[32] yet many see manifest in the superhero cult the qualities of individualism and the collective identity of WASP America which went on the offensive in the McCarthyite and

Cold War period. Eco's perception of the new middle ages involves the recognition that cultural space is permeable, that – unlike the watertight 'Empire' – the host culture is subject to influences from outside itself that are beyond its control. *The Dark Knight Returns* and *Watchmen* are two comics which seem to take this cultural 'permeability' as their starting point for their reconstruction of superhero ideology.

This, it could be argued, is where the superhero acts out his role in the game of cultural semiotics. Like most important signs, the superhero supports a varied and contradictory battery of readings. He is both the exotic and the agent of order which brings the exotic to book. His costume marks him out as a proponent of change and exoticism, yet he surprises us by his adherance to an almost archaic code of personal honour. As with superhero sexuality, the unpredictable nature of contemporary culture is adduced through a play of visual signs in order more effectively to relegate it to the domain of things one has learned how to control.

This may be why the superhero and supervillain exist so comfortably in the same social space, converse on familiar terms, and wear similar style costumes when battling each other. They represent the inferred challenge to the social order (Eco's Barbarians) and the means of survival – through the exposition of virtues that might have been considered to be past their prime. The superhero by his very existence asserts American utopianism, which remains (as has been ably pointed out by Baudrillard in *America*)[33] a highly potent cultural myth. The exciting developments in superhero comics over the last decade or so have largely been the product of writers and artists who have come to understand and work around or through the superhero's cultural iconography – using the myth of the superhero to make a calculated statement about the culture which the myth attempts to comprehend.

4 Three Key Texts

X-Men 108–143

The original X-Men were launched in 1964, as part of the explosion of new ideas and titles that emerged from Marvel under the editorship of Stan Lee. The exciting new ingredient in the Marvel superheroes of the 1960s was the quality of irony, coupled with the openly anti-heroic nature of many of the lead characters. The tone was in many ways set by two key new superheroes. The first of these was the arrogant, quarrelsome, short-tempered and genuinely ugly Thing – aka the likable and dependable Benjamin Grimm of the Stan Lee/Jack Kirby *Fantastic Four*. The other keynote superhero was Spider-Man, as originally written by Stan Lee and drawn by Steve Ditko. Both of these titles used an ironic stance to comment on the superhero identity and alter-ego of their characters, integrating the anti-heroic alter-ego with the all-conquering hero and thus creating the 'hero with problems', which carried the superhero comic several steps beyond the Clark Kent/Superman duality in terms of literary characterization. The Lee/Ditko Spider-Man stories are possibly the clearest demonstration of this principle – the more so because Ditko's spiky artwork and attenuated figures (the opposite of Kirby's blocky but dynamic style)[1] all cut across the expectations of readers schooled in the 1950s and early 1960s DC artists such as Sheldon Moldoff and Wayne Boring.[2]

The underlying concept of the *X-Men* took these new qualities of doubt and irony one stage further – by building distrust and suspicion into the very fabric of the continuity. The X-Men were mutants: young men and women who possessed extraordinary powers. These powers set them apart from the rest of humanity, although born as normal children to normal parents. The appearance of such a strain of mutants is explained as being the result of increased radiation in the earth's atmosphere. Mutants are therefore 'children of the atom' – by-products of Cold War nuclear testing. Their mutant powers lie dormant until puberty – at which point they suddenly begin to manifest themselves.

The physical appearance of mutants can sometimes be disturbing, and any display of their powers is a potentially terrifying experience for bystanders. Small wonder then that the X-Men – a team of young mutant superheroes assembled by wheelchair-bound middle-aged mutant Professor Charles Xavier – are 'hated and feared by the world they have sworn to protect.'

The original X-Men – Cyclops, Marvel Girl, Angel, The Beast and Iceman – ran to 66 issues, with a further 27 issues of reprinted material occupying *X-Men* 67–93. As a group of teenagers, some orphaned (Cyclops) and several with bizarre physical characteristics (Angel, The Beast, Cyclops), the X-Men became a very close-knit super-team, clustering deferentially around their middle-aged mentor and father-figure, Professor Xavier. Often, well-coordinated teamwork would allow the X-Men to defeat seemingly more powerful villains such as the well-nigh unstoppable Juggernaut. But the X-Men's arch nemesis remained Magneto, Master of Magnetism and chief of the 'Brotherhood of Evil Mutants' – an inversion of the X-Men and an organization dedicated to the use of mutant powers to dominate 'inferior' homo sapiens.[3]

The original X-Men are a subject enough in themselves. But the best was yet to come. On the revival of the comic in 1974[4] (*Giant Size X-Men* 1), Chris Claremont took over as writer. There was a dramatic change in the composition of the team. Out went the Angel, Beast and Iceman and – initially – Marvel Girl (Jean Grey), with her telekinetic powers and her smouldering romance with Scott (Cyclops) Summers. In place of these characters came a new, international line-up, consisting of a teleporting blue German elf (Nightcrawler), a muscular Russian who could transform his body into 'living steel' (Colossus), an African Goddess with mutant power over the elements (Storm), an Irish ex-villain with a powerful 'sonic-scream' (Banshee), a mutant Apache with speed, agility and tracking skills (Thunderbird – soon killed off), and a psychopathic pint-sized Canadian with unbreakable 'adamantium' bones, plus claws which popped out of his knuckles (Wolverine). Cyclops remained on the team as Professor Xavier's deputy and field commander. A more weird and varied group of superheroes had never been seen.

The new *X-Men* quickly became Marvel's most popular title – both in terms of sales and critical appreciation. The comic's popularity lifted even higher when John Byrne took over the artwork in 1977.[5] This was Byrne's first big assignment, and his detailed but cinematic style was ideal for such a fast moving and complex team comic. Together with inker Terry Austin, Byrne and Claremont remained together on the *X-Men* until late 1980: *X-Men* 108–109 and 111–143. These issues are generally considered to be one of the high points of monthly superhero comics.

Byrne's artwork meshes very effectively with Austin's inking and the moody, expressive colouring of Glynis Wein. The switch of artist from Dave Cockrum to Byrne changed the whole style and narrative approach of the comic – an obvious example is the complete visual transformation Byrne wrought on Wolverine. Byrne's style of artwork seemed to act as the ideal springboard for Claremont to develop the characterization at a deeper level than anything seen in a team superhero comic before. Comics are the result of collective effort, and nothing demonstrates this principle better than the Byrne/Claremont/Austin/Wein *X-Men*.

One of the main elements which gave the Byrne/Claremont *X-Men* an extra dimension compared with other material of the period was the continuing use of unresolved conflicts between the individual characters, which outlasted any individual plot-line and were the main driving force of the comic's development. These unresolved conflicts were not presented as arising from any specific misunderstandings or disagreements. They were portrayed as inseparable from the life of a superhero team. The most notable conflict, which set the tone for many of the Byrne/Claremont issues, was that between the longtime X-Man and team leader Cyclops (Scott Summers), and the unpredictable newcomer Wolverine. Cockrum's Wolverine had been awkward and confrontational, but after Byrne's arrival the character began to round out and attract a considerable fan following. Wolverine offered a permanent challenge to Cyclops's style of leadership that was rooted in a wholly different view of what a superhero was meant to be. To expedite this shifting perspective on the story, Byrne employed a style of sequential art that was 'cinematic' in the sense that it constantly interpreted each panel and each segment of the narrative from an implied and subjective point of view. The reader was drawn in, invited to take sides in the characters' conflicts.

Byrne certainly offers occasional bravura displays and double page splashes, but these are always paced to punctuate the story at key turning points – such as the splash page of the Petrified Man's city in *X-Men* 116, the appearance of Sauron on *X-Men* 115, or the first full view of Alpha Flight in *X-Men* 121.[6] Byrne's pages of artwork have a fluidity and rhythm which helps the reader into the subjective identification with one character or another which is part of the enjoyment of a team comic. Each character's point of view can be played up as required. Byrne's skill with the 'camera angles' involves and includes the reader in the construction of the narrative. A simple example can be found on pages 3–4 of *X-Men* 122.

Colossus is undergoing a test of his strength in the X-Men's 'Danger Room' – the gadget-packed training gymnasium in Charles Xavier's Westchester County mansion where the team hone and refine their fighting skills. Colossus is unsure of his value to the team after failures in battle with Magneto, whose control of magnetic forces has made Colossus vulnerable to his attack and a danger to the rest of the team. Colossus is being tested between the walls of a

Page 3, *The Uncanny X-Men* 122, © Marvel Entertainment Group, Inc. 1979.

hydraulic press – and he's failing the test. Wolverine, impatient as ever with Cyclops's leadership, shorts out the control panel and steps into the Danger Room himself. Page 3 panel 1 shows Wolverine from Colossus's point of view. The reader can see Colossus's head and shoulders, but the angle of vision is from inside the hydraulic press: the reader looks out, sharing Colossus's ordeal. Panel 2 pulls back to reveal Colossus's arms, strained and bent, struggling to use their full strength. Wolverine, with exaggerated difficulty, is crawling inside the hydraulic press. The reader's view of him is once again Colossus's, but the panel's art links the two characters together via Wolverine's outstretched hand.

Panel 3 moves to a close-up, Colossus at the right, under great pressure, Wolverine casually sharing his danger, lighting a cigarette. Now Wolverine speaks his mind.

> I got an idea what's buggin' you, pal. Most of us were loners 'fore we became X-Men. The Team's kinda given us the family we never had. But you got family, friends, roots.[7]

The background to this panel is the steel grey of the press, poised to crush both characters. Panel 4 cuts to Cyclops/Scott Summers in the control room. 'The press is at full power, Colossus! Either you stop it on your own . . . or you'll both be squashed!'

Colossus breaks loose in panel 5 with devastating effect. Wolverine, his task of motivating Colossus accomplished, leaps clear with nonchalant agility. Colossus's effort to push back the clamps forces them up against the panel borders, and the artwork's diagonals carry the reader's eye away from the central figures to the off-centre speech balloon, loosely connected to Wolverine by way of an arrow a good inch-and-a-half from the speaker. The balloon is drawn in the zig-zag outline that denotes a shouted or highly emotive utterance:

> Way to go, Russkie!

Colossus's immense strength is established and given a context. Wolverine's encouraging shout places him firmly in the team – 'way to go'. But 'Russkie' also reminds us that the X-Men are an ethnic patchwork, exotic in every sense of the word. Their unity embraces the greatest possible diversity. Colossus's powers may be extraordinary, but, as with the rest of us, they are linked to his overall morale. This is a key to many X-Men confrontations – the 'extra effort' is almost always a factor, the mutant ability of each character is rarely enough on its own – it must be applied with high morale and fighting spirit. So, for example, the non-Byrne but Claremont-scripted *X-Men* 150 pits the X-Men against arch-foe Magneto with their mutant abilities totally out of commission: the supreme test of the 'extra effort'. They come through triumphantly.

Page 5 is an altogether quieter page of artwork. Panel 1 is objective and expository. Cyclops is mobile, erupting into the panel from the right. Wolverine and Colossus are in repose on the damaged apparatus. The tableau effect continues to group Wolverine and Colossus together – seen now in the same panel as Cyclops, they are nevertheless divided from him by the corner of the hydraulic apparatus and the Danger Room, which forms a vertical line dividing the panel in two. Panels 2 and 3 show Cyclops in conflict with Wolverine, who leans out of panel 2 as Cyclops tells him to repair the damage to the control panel. Cyclops stands in front of a curious red circle, which could be a window from the control panel into the Danger Room. Its main function, however, is to draw attention to Scott's head, which dominates the panel with a rather laboured and formal authority. Panel 3 shows Colossus and Cyclops from the back as they turn away, with Wolverine effectively alongside Scott, but divided by the panel border. As in panel 1, this technique highlights the constant tension between Cyclops and Wolverine, together but never companions. Wolverine is holding the tool-kit that Scott offered him in the previous panel, but the reader never sees it pass from one hand to the other.

Panel 4 takes us out of the Danger Room and fixes on another character's point of view – that of Colleen Wing, Scott's romantic interest for the present. Panel 5 gives a tight view of Colleen over Cyclops's shoulder, fending away her inviting smile with his stolid half-head and shoulder. This mirrors the exchange in the dialogue:

> H'lo sailor . . . New in town?
>
> Hi yourself, Colleen.

Panel 6 is still more subjective, as Cyclops's speech balloon is directed outside the panel, while the reader sees Colleen Wing more or less from Cyclops's point of view, framed by Cyclops's arm, pressing the intercom to call Banshee and set up the action of the next page. Nevertheless, it is Scott/Cyclops who is the object of our gaze in both panels 5 and 6. We look at him from one side and meet the eyes of Colleen looking from the other. Her affectionate smile is a clear response to the subtext between the two characters, and owes nothing to Cyclops's dry, expository dialogue. Not so strange then, that, by the end of the comic, Colleen is handing Scott the key to her door in an envelope as she leaves town on the train.

Byrne publicly identified himself with the character and attitudes of Wolverine, Claremont with the rest of the X-Men team.[8] Whilst the external action of the comic proceeded as a series of encounters

Page 5, *The Uncanny X-Men* 122, © Marvel Entertainment Group, Inc. 1979.

between the X-Men and various menaces to society (Magneto, Arcade, The Hellfire Club and so on), the unresolved action of the continuity was largely bound up with this debate over the nature of heroic or noble action. On several occasions (beginning with *X-Men* 108, Byrne's first issue) the implication was made that the X-Men formed some kind of Gestalt entity, of which the whole was greater than the sum of the parts. Byrne and Claremont also introduced Cabbalistic notions about the mystic Tree of Life into the script, to flesh out the Gestalt mutant group theme – which can itself be traced back to Theodore Sturgeon's novel *More Than Human*.[9] This theme comes to the fore during the sequence where Jean Grey, now the virtually all-powerful Phoenix, patches up a gap in the fabric of space-time and thereby saves the universe as we know it from destruction.

> She [Phoenix] reaches out, images cascading through her mind, thoughts and feelings becoming tangible – she touching them, they her – the patterns of her life, of the X-Men's lives, becoming one with the lattice pattern surrounding the N-Galaxy.
>
> . . . In that instant she feels her power, the power of her friends, sing within her; as she re-energizes the energy lattice – it's as if a door has opened before her eyes.
>
> A new pattern forms – shaped like the mystic tree of life – with Xavier its lofty crown and Colossus its base. Each X-Man has a place, each a purpose greater than himself or herself.[10]

This type of pop-mysticism is less interesting for itself than for what it tells us about Byrne and Claremont's intentions concerning the narrative structure of the comic as a whole. Many of the stories that follow in the Byrne/Claremont sequence deal with the themes expressed in this text passage, but in a less pretentious manner: leadership, loyalty, group dynamics, trust, individual and collective action.

X-Men 111–113 sees arch-enemy Magneto capture the X-Men and neutralize both their mutant powers and the normal control of their nervous systems over their bodies. They escape and battle Magneto a second time, winning on this occasion through perfect coordination and teamwork. *X-Men* 120–121 finds them in Canada, coming up against Canada's new superhero team, Alpha Flight. Alpha Flight's aim is to recapture Wolverine – once part of Alpha Flight's development programme. The X-Men pair off and battle one-on-one with the most appropriate opponent in the hostile team – appropriate, that is, in the sense of having the most similar superpowers. The battle is interrupted when a snowstorm created by one of the Alpha Flight team to divert the X-Men's plane gets out of control and threatens to destroy half of Canada. Storm breaks off the fight to put a stop to the blizzard. This achieved, the two superteams are ready to return to the fray, but Wolverine offers to surrender himself to the Canadian authorities in return for the X-Men's safe passage back to the USA. Cyclops is taken aback by the offer, but agrees. Subsequently (on the next page) Wolverine turns up in the X-Men's plane flying back to New York, having escaped from a special Wolverine-proof armoured car. His sacrifice has worked to preserve the unity of the team.

X-Men 122–124 sees a three-part battle with Arcade, a non-superpowered assassin who has constructed a murderous amusement park employing numerous motifs from popular culture; pinball, arcade games, bumper cars, models of supervillains. The main theme of this sequence, however, is the brainwashing of Colossus by phoney KGB agent Colonel Alexei Vazhin (a creation of Arcade) and his temporary transformation into the Proletarian – 'Workers' Hero of the Soviet Union'. Vazhin interrogates Colossus against a barrage of blinding lights:

> . . . What loyal son of Mother Russia offers his services, and his superpowers, to a team based in the United States?[11]

Temporarily convinced by Vazhin's argument, Colossus is brainwashed into attacking his team-mates, to the immense glee of the crazily malignant Arcade – 'O Boy – This is great!'. Arcade, a rich kid from Beverly Hills who killed his own father to grab his inheritance and set himself up as an assassin for hire is quite clearly an embodiment of everything a stock KGB figure such as Vazhin should be fulminating against.[12] And Arcade's murderous operations make use of just about every item that spells junk-culture 'America' to the outside world: there is even a suggestion of the Stars and Stripes in the colour scheme of his suit and stack shoes. Once again (as in the Phoenix/collapsing galaxy story) the X-Men triumph through their group loyalty. Colossus grabs Storm and Cyclops and is strangling them one in each hand; they appeal to his sense of family, already addressed by Wolverine in the Danger Room sequence from *X-Men* 122. Storm begins

> When I was a little girl, I grew up alone . . . no family, no real friends . . . that all changed when I joined the X-Men.

Cyclops joins in:

> It changed for us all, Peter. The X-Men is more than just a school for mutants . . . Deep down, you must know that! We're . . . almost like a family, I guess.[13]

***X-Men* 124, page 26. The family loyalty of the X-Men proves stronger than Colossus's brainwashing at the hands of the villainous Arcade. *The Uncanny X-Men* 124, © Marvel Entertainment Group, Inc. 1979.**

The appeal works, Colossus snaps out of it. In the next major storyline, he gets to deliver the *coup de grace* to the exceptionally dangerous and malevolent mutant Proteus.

Dwelling on Wolverine, Cyclops and Colossus is all too easy, as they stand out as the big successes of the Byrne/Claremont X-Men, along with the development of Jean Grey into Phoenix and beyond – Jean, like Cyclops, being a character left over from the original X-Men cycle. Nightcrawler and Storm were less completely realized characters. Nightcrawler was effectively a minor member of the team, a humorous and effective eccentric, the joker of the outfit, the friendly devil with the blue face and the smell of brimstone when he teleported; an acceptable supporting character. Storm – mutant Goddess from Africa with power over the elements – was a more ambitious and original creation, and, comparatively, a less successful one.

Storm enjoyed a period as leader of the X-Men after Byrne's departure, and is clearly a character dear to Claremont's heart. She is certainly an exciting and original creation – her powers have great visual appeal, and her long white hair and dark complexion provide the kind of contrasting visual image that gives credibility to the underlying pretext of the mutant theme. Storm – despite her name – is on all occasions an advocate of calm and the healing of divisions – within the X-Men team or outside it. In the battle with Alpha Flight she brings the entire Canadian weather pattern back under control. Inside the collapsing N-Galaxy she is the first to offer her 'life force' as a psychic anchor to Phoenix, saving the day for the entire universe. When young mutant Kitty Pride appears on the scene, Storm takes her in hand.

Storm is also a focus for the opposing themes and mythologies which the X-Men embody; her character reconciles a whole gamut of conflicting myths and ideologies. An elemental force of nature, she is the least spontaneous and most withdrawn of the X-Men. Asexual (even for a superheroine) she sports perhaps the most revealing and fetishistic black costume of any 1970s Marvel or DC character. As with the Scarlet Witch (see page 80), Storm's exotic sexuality is offered in the context of family and domestic life: the family being in this case the X-Men themselves.[14] She occupies a quasi-maternal role in the dynamics of the group, distantly tolerant of the flirtatious sexuality of Nightcrawler or Wolverine. Subsequent development of the character notwithstanding, Storm's chief function in the Byrne/Claremont X-Men was to reconcile contradictions, a traditionally female role. Arguably, even her impressive superpowers reflect this function, embodying as they do the forces of nature which are enveloping rather than explosive or lacerating in their effect. Despite the fashionable elements that went into her characterization, Storm reflects many of the traditional solutions to devising a female superhero in a team context.

Byrne and Claremont's run on the *X-Men* embraces, by good planning and good fortune, various major character developments that span the length of their collaboration. Marvel Girl (Jean Grey) becomes Phoenix, gains immense power, consumates her love for Cyclops, is tempted and corrupted by the Hellfire Club into becoming their Black Queen, and finally dies in a staged battle to determine her guilt in destroying an entire solar system when on the loose as the Dark Phoenix – the disastrous result of the Hellfire Club's meddling with her mind.[15] Colossus, in the meantime, establishes his trust and confidence in the team, Nightcrawler comes to accept his strange appearance within the security offered by the X-Men; Wolverine and Cyclops arrive at an uneasy compromise without ever resolving Wolverine's implicit challenge to Cyclops's leadership of the team. When Cyclops departs in *X-Men* 138, it is Storm who takes over leadership of the team. It was this unwavering consistency of character development which, at the time of publication, set the Byrne/Claremont *X-Men* up as a model of how a team superhero comic should be conducted. But the *X-Men* was still constrained by the demands of continuity and consistency with its back issues and the rest of the Marvel universe. *The Dark Knight Returns* and *Watchmen*, the second and third key texts, are self-contained graphic novels: which, as much as any other single feature, explains the scope of their break with the traditional way of doing things.

The Dark Knight Returns

There are similarities between *The Dark Knight Returns* and *Watchmen*: they have often been bracketed together as representing a common point of evolution in the superhero story – and not just by critics: Miller and Moore have both commented on the parallels that exist between their works. Both are the product of writers and artists of a broadly similar age and generation within the comics industry. Frank Miller's work was first published by Marvel in 1979 (*Daredevil* 158), and Alan Moore's first scripts for *Doctor Who Weekly* and *2000AD* appeared in the same year.

There are further links between the two works, both implicit and explicit. Miller and Moore both enjoyed a meteoric rise through the ranks of comic-book writers and writer-artists, but neither has been happy with the imposed limitation of the 32-page monthly superhero comic, though they have both achieved notable work within the format. Both *Dark Knight* and *Watchmen* are conscious attempts to up the stakes and raise the overall status and cultural prestige of the superhero genre and the comic-book medium as a whole. Paradoxically, this has in practice meant producing works which partly if not wholly attack the basis and the assumptions of the genre of which they are ostensibly a part. Reviewers have not been tardy to grab at such terms as 'post modernist' comic-books to assimilate the process of self-criticism to which the highly self-conscious Miller and Moore subject the superhero genre.

The bid for increased cultural credibility is apparent as soon as you pick up a copy of the perfect-bound paperback graphic novel reprinting of either title. Although initially published as a limited-run series, both titles form single, complete texts which stand alone as single, complete volumes. They bind up into fairly substantial books, and often elicit the response from the uncommitted reader: 'I didn't know there were comics like these.' The cover designs of both titles are clearly intended to reinforce such an impression, with moody, spare graphics which totally bypass the convention of sensationalizing the contents of the comic. *The Dark Knight* lists Miller, Janson and Varley on the front cover, and also announces an 'Introduction by Alan Moore' – yet another link between *The Dark Knight* and *Watchmen*. The back cover of *Dark Knight* features a moody photograph of Frank Miller and a quote from Stephen King: '. . . probably the finest piece of comic art ever to be published in a popular edition . . .' Titan Books' British edition of *Watchmen* likewise lists Moore and Gibbons on the front cover, with further moody photographs of both men on the back, together with review quotes from four sources: *The Face* ('Stretches the horizons of the graphic novel'), *The Independent* ('One of the harbingers of the new wave . . . [which] created a new readership for comics among adults . . .), *Q* ('The most advanced comic yet . . .') and *Time Out* ('A phenonemon . . . a legitimate novel . . . the first series in nearly thirty years to assume that comic reading doesn't stop with the advent of adolescence').

Strong stuff: it hardly comes as a surprise that both books are printed on high-quality paper, and that there are no adverts for x-ray binoculars and Charles Atlas body-building courses lurking inside. The sheer number of ways in which both graphic novels belie popular conceptions of the comic-book medium can be appreciated best in a table of binary opposites:

Traditional Four-Colour Comics	***Dark Knight/Watchmen***
Thin	Thick
Wire-stitched	Perfect-bound
Dramatic, action cover	Enigmatic, low-key cover

No listing of author/artist on cover	Name of author/artist on cover, plus photos
Reviews irrelevant	Quotes reviews on cover
Cheap paper	High-quality paper
Adverts on alternate spreads	No adverts
Periodical	Book
Cheap	Expensive

The last line is perhaps the most important of all. The presentation of both *Dark Knight* and *Watchmen* being as it is – with the implicit encouragement to treat both titles as serious, adult fiction – predicates a price equal to a mass-market illustrated book, not a down-market news-stand item. At £10 a copy, comics can't just be for the kids.[16]

Nor are these raised expectations disappointed by the texts. Both use certain common strategies which perform both the function of raising the intellectual and cultural stakes and articulating narrative themes and ideological positions. Firstly, *Dark Knight* and *Watchmen* are intensely media-aware. *Dark Knight*, for example, employs over and over again the inserted TV screen as a panel in its own right. The television panels provide an incessant commentary on the developing narrative of Batman's return to crime fighting.[17] By containing television so adroitly, *Dark Knight* asserts the legitimacy of its passing comment on the medium's inanity (sweet revenge for the smug TV talk shows condemning comic-books as illiterate garbage). American television is held up to scrutiny and abrasive ridicule centring on its pomposity and grandiloquence: the reckless self-confidence which allows TV show hosts to posture as unacknowledged legislators is most tellingly parodied in the sequence where the Joker is released from a mental asylum and lionized on a late-night chat show. The text of *Dark Knight* also demonstrates how TV news drugs the public's sensibilities into accepting violence as part of everyday life through its proximity to 'balancing' good news – as in, for example, the close-up of Bruce Wayne's hand on the TV remote control intercut on page (a) 16 with news images from several different channels:

> 'four killed in a senseless attack on . . .'
> '. . . subway deaths reached an all-time high this . . .'
> '. . . rape and mutilation of . . .'
> '. . . here's Dave with some good news. Dave?'
> 'Right, Lola. Right as rain. The heat's finally gonna break . . . but we're in for a whopper of a . . .'[18]

Interviews with 'members of the public' in news reporting also come in for a hammering, as in (a) 37:

> A. Batman? Yeah, I think he's a-okay. He's kicking just the right butts – butts the cops ain't kicking, that's for sure. Hope he goes after the homos next.
>
> B. Makes me sick. We must treat the socially misoriented with rehabilitative methods. We must patiently realign their – excuse me – ? No, I'd never live in the city . . .[19]

The Joker, released from mental hospital into an appearance on the 'David Endochrine Show', systematically slaughters over 200 members of the studio audience, including fellow chat-show guests and the psychiatrist who approved his release. When limited nuclear war breaks out in the last chapter of *Dark Knight*, the electromagnetic pulse of the single nuclear weapon detonated, wipes out (amongst other things) all TV broadcasts. The jailed members of the Mutant gang – social deviants of the most violent kind – riot and kill two prison guards. No TV is the last straw.

Watchmen concentrates its satire on the printed media, parodying news chatter from a garrulous news vendor, a right-wing fanatic journalist (Hector Godfrey, editor of the *New Frontiersman*), and 'right-on' magazines (*Nova Express*, edited by Doug Roth). The caricatured knee-jerk reaction of these journalists to the superheroes they report on pokes fun at the (real) news media's presumptions to judge the superhero genre as a less than worthy art-form. Ex-superhero Adrian Veidt's wall of TV screens – which he uses to monitor world trends and their impact on his business empire – are mainly tuned in to advertisements. Clearly Veidt regards these as a more reliable source of information than the babble of news commentary.[20]

If *Dark Knight* takes revenge on TV with one hand, with the other it hunts down that other arch-enemy of the comics medium, the social scientist. Miller's chief satirical Aunt Sally here is Dr Bartholomew Wolper, psychiatrist to both Two-Face and the Joker, and instrumental in obtaining their release. Wolper campaigns tirelessly for the arrest of Batman:

> You see, it all gets down to this Batman fellow. Batman's psychotic sublimative/psycho erotic behavior pattern is like a net. Weak-egoed neurotics, like Harvey, are drawn into corresponding intersticing patterns. You might say Batman commits the crimes . . . using his so-called villains as narcissistic proxies . . .[21]

***The Dark Knight Returns*, page (a) 8. One of the most sustained uses of the TV screen image as panel. Two-Face's doctor and psychiatrist announce his mental and physical healing.**

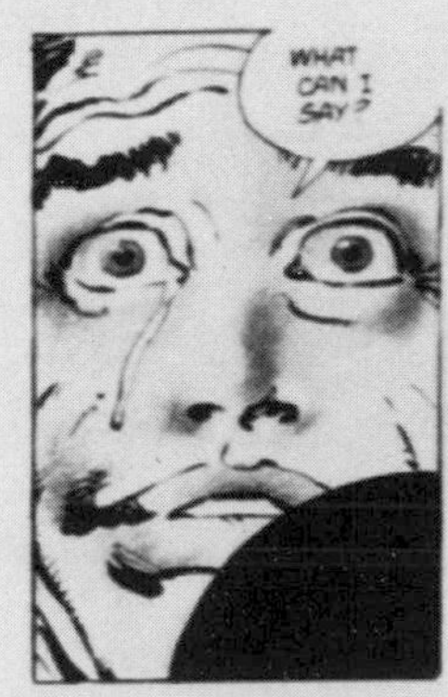
WHAT CAN I SAY?

...THANK YOU, TOM. A NEW LIFE BEGINS TODAY FOR HARVEY DENT.

DENT, A FORMER DISTRICT ATTORNEY, BECAME OBSESSED WITH THE NUMBER TWO WHEN HALF HIS FACE WAS SCARRED BY ACID.

DENT BELIEVED HIS DISFIGURATION REVEALED A HIDDEN, EVIL SIDE TO HIS NATURE. HE ADOPTED AS HIS PERSONAL SYMBOL A DOLLAR COIN...

...ONE SIDE OF WHICH WAS DEFACED, TO REPRESENT THE WARRING SIDES OF HIS SPLIT-PERSONALITY. A FLIP OF THE COIN COULD MEAN LIFE OR DEATH FOR HIS VICTIMS.

DENT'S CRIMES WERE BRILLIANTLY PATHOLOGICAL, THE MOST HORRENDOUS OF WHICH WAS HIS LAST--

--THE KIDNAPPING AND RANSOMING OF SIAMESE TWINS, ONE OF WHOM HE ATTEMPTED TO MURDER EVEN AFTER THE RANSOM WAS PAID.

HE WAS APPREHENDED IN THE ACT BY GOTHAM'S FAMOUS VIGILANTE, THE BATMAN, AND COMMITTED TO ARKHAM ASYLUM TWELVE YEARS AGO.

FOR THE PAST THREE YEARS DENT HAS BEEN TREATED BY DR. BARTHOLOMEW WOLPER FOR HIS PSYCHOSIS...

...WHILE NOBEL PRIZE-WINNING PLASTIC SURGEON DR. HERBERT WILLING DEDICATED HIMSELF TO RESTORING THE FACE OF HARVEY DENT.

SPEAKING TODAY, BOTH DOCTORS WERE JUBILANT.

HARVEY'S READY TO LOOK AT THE WORLD AND SAY, "HEY--I'M OKAY."

AND HE LOOKS GREAT.

DENT READ A BRIEF STATEMENT TO THE MEDIA...

I DO NOT ASK GOTHAM CITY TO FORGIVE MY CRIMES. I MUST EARN THAT, BY DEDICATING MYSELF TO PUBLIC SERVICE.

FOR ME, THIS IS THE END OF A LONG NIGHTMARE... AND THE FIRST STEP ON THE LONG ROAD TO ABSOLUTION.

and later

> Picture the public psyche as a vast, moist membrane – through the media, Batman has struck this membrane a vicious blow, and it has recoiled. Hence your misleading statistics. But you see, Ted, the membrane is flexible – and permeable. Here the more significant effects of the blow become calculable, even predictable. To wit – every anti-social act can be traced to an irresponsible media input. Given this, the presence of such an aberrant, violent force in the media can only lead to anti-social programming.[22]

Alan Moore's introduction to *Dark Knight* concentrates on the theme of heroism: 'heroes are starting to become rather a problem.' *The Dark Knight Returns* is a story about the social consensus that permits heroes to operate, and its apparent breakdown. This is one reason why the story couldn't have been told as part of continuity, as continuity presupposes the existence of some form of ideological consensus, if only between the creators and the fans. But one of the intentions of *Dark Knight*, as Moore points out in his introduction, is to take all the familiar and received ingredients of the Batman continuity – Robin, the Batmobile, Commissioner Gordon – and situate them in a text that radically restructures their meaning. So, Robin becomes a thirteen-year-old girl and Batman is accused of child endangerment; the Batmobile is transformed into a massive armoured personnel carrier; Commissioner Gordon is displaced by a much younger policewoman who proceeds to put out a warrant for Batman's arrest.

A still more profound change is in the portrayal of the villains and their relationship to the rest of society. The Joker and the Penguin go to jail in Batman stories of the 1940s with an 'it's a fair cop, guv' attitude which acknowledges the deviant nature of their activities, and the justice of the alliance between Batman (the vigilante) and Commissioner Gordon (as the law) in combining to catch and punish them. In material from the 1940s to the 1960s, the villains are isolated menaces with no support within society at large, and no recourse to widespread sympathy.

Beginning in the 1970s, and accelerating in the 1980s, the consensus view of society began to crumble in many superhero stories. Captain America's disgust over the Watergate affair, his resignation and return to action as the anonymous Nomad, are early examples (1974–75) of this process at work. The journey from Captain America, a composite icon of the American Flag, and military, national and democratic zeal, to the identity-denying Nomad – one who literally has no home – is an easy one to interpret against the background of post-Watergate, post-Vietnam America. But Captain America's soul searching odyssey led eventually to a re-establishment of consensus – continuity demanded nothing less. It was, however, a more questioning and politically conscious interpretation of his role in relation to political authority, and Steve Englehart's Nomad cycle started a trend for superhero stories in which the political underpinning for superhero actions was examined.[23] In *Dark Knight* this questioning has reached a point where there are no longer any (offered) solutions.

Dark Knight opens with Bruce Wayne retired from his Batman identity for some ten years, continuing to lead the life of a respectable playboy/industrialist – but without the companionship of Dick Grayson, Jason Todd or Tim Drake, the three Robins. Outside the old-money portals of Wayne Mansion, Gotham City is in a bad way, with spiralling crime, gangsterism, and threats against the life of about-to-retire Police Commissioner Gordon. Attacked by members of the Mutant Gang at the spot where his parents were shot down before his eyes all those years before, and mentally besieged by media reports of violent crime, Wayne decides to go back into action as the Batman – despite now being aged in his mid-fifties. He encounters long-time villains Two Face and the Joker, as well as the Mutants, a stylishly dressed gang of youths who go in for ultra-violence along the lines of Alex and his Droogs in *A Clockwork Orange*. Batman defeats the leader of the Mutants in single combat: many of the gang then transfer their allegiance and rename themselves the 'Sons of the Batman', painting their faces with bat-silhouettes and carrying out violent vigilante actions against Gotham's criminal elements. Superman – unmarked by the passage of time – is called in by the government to bring Batman under control. Their final confrontation takes place against a backdrop of near-total social breakdown, as a Soviet nuclear warhead unleashed in a regional conflict in Central America causes a magnetic pulse which disrupts all electrical communication and throws up a blanket of cloud cover over North America. After faking his own death, Batman leads his small army of ex-Mutant gang members, plus his new-found Robin, down into the caves below the Batcave: '. . . an army . . . to bring sense to a world plagued by worse than thieves and murderers.'

In a TV interview, Miller has mentioned some of the personal experiences that influenced the crafting of *Dark Knight*.[24] He speaks of life in New York in the 1980s – 'a place that's silly and frightening at the same time. I hope people find *Dark Knight* both silly and frightening . . .' Deviance has become the norm. Consensus has been attacked to the point where there are no longer any clear normative values. Miller takes this as his starting point, and works up a series of variations on the theme. So, the Joker, murderer of over 600 victims, is made into a media star on his release from Arkham Asylum. The Joker becomes just one more oddball to be repackaged as entertainment, by a TV network clearly claiming a liberal broad-mindedness as the alibi for its uncritical inclusiveness. The smug faces of Endochrine and his sidekick announce their star guest:

> What can I say about our next guest that hasn't been said before? Paul?
>
> He's a kook, Dave. A maniac. A real lunatic. No, I mean it. He's a nut . . .
>
> You're said to have only killed about six hundred people, Joker. Now don't take this the wrong way, but I think you've been holding out on us.[25]

Social disintegration is also embodied in the text's use of proliferating and ambiguous signs – both explicit and implicit (the same is also true of *Watchmen*). Batman, the 'social fascist', finds himself battling a psychopathic and androgynous gang leader who wears swastikas on his/her breasts and buttocks, plus a flat-top hairstyle and Liza Minnelli long gloves. Signs determine individuals as normal or deviant. Later on, during the nuclear alert and black-out a priest encounters a youth dressed like the members of the Mutant gang – but this youth turns out to be a hero during the ensuing panic and rioting. Pro- and anti-Batman lobbies appear on TV fronting logos reminiscent of the posters for the movie *Ghostbusters*. Is Batman the social menace, the menaced, or a symptom of social division? Batman's escape from newly-appointed Police Commissioner Ellen Yindel's men brings a charge against the Caped Crusader of child endangerment: as TV's Lola Chong puts it 'Batman has been sighted using a young boy as a shield against police gunfire.' 'Boy Wonder – got to be' comments a viewer. Except, of course, that it's a girl.[26]

Ellen Yindel replaces James Gordon as Gotham's Police Commissioner around half way through *Dark Knight*. Gordon is way overdue for retirement, and the debate over who should succeed him is yet another debate about the political use of signs. Gallagher (Police Media Director) and the Mayor discuss the options:

> Gordon's popular
>
> I know that. Don't you think I know that? And I've given it a lot of thought. Dale's looking good to me. He's available . . . and he's black . . .
>
> Black's passé, your honor. Besides, Dale's neutral on the Batman thing. And you know what your own neutrality is costing you . . .

> I'm not neutral. Who says I'm neutral? I'm conflicted.[27]

A black commissioner as a sign of social unity is passé: the public see through the trick. What Gallagher fixes on is a tough woman from Chicago with a brilliant arrest record and a jaw-line to rival Clark Kent's. All is corrupt: all motives are conflicted. The media – the public – can only be seduced by an appropriate play of signs.

Batman is more than just a superhero: he is also the sign of a superhero. Batman represents comics and the whole superhero genre: to tell a story of corruption and moral reversal with Batman as its protagonist is altogether different from starting with the blank slate of a new character. Batman is a sign invested with so many layers of meaning that each separate reversal of the use of that sign is an attention-grabbing narrative event. Miller himself has commented:

> He's a character you can describe in a few seconds. His parents were murdered in front of his eyes when he was a kid – he's warring on crime for the rest of his life . . . And he looks great! And the whole character is so simple, that it's open to the widest variety of treatments and interpretations.

'The World only makes sense if you force it to.' The broken consensus offers only fragmentary experience, crime, fetishism, casual bigotry, drugs, alcohol, private discourse in street slang ('Rad', 'Balls Rad', 'Balls Nasty', shrill the Mutant gang). It's a world overcharged with meaning, over-determined by signs. At the end of their fight to the death the Joker and Batman are linked together visually in a near-sexual embrace (c) 46–47 while Batman's final roof-top confrontation with Two-Face (a) 47 shows explicitly that the two characters have become a mirror for each other:

> Take a look . . . have your laugh. I'm fixed all right. At least both sides match . . . have your laugh, Batman . . . take a look! . . . Take a look . . .
>
> [I close my eyes and listen. Not fooled by sight I see him . . .as he is. I see him. I see]
>
> I see . . . a reflection, Harvey. A reflection.[28]

The skilful interplay of image and text takes this assertion beyond simple rhetoric. In a Gotham City over-determined by signs, where consensus is no longer available, Batman and Two Face are able to decode a certain meaning in each other's opposition. Without supervillains there would be no Batman, or at any rate, no meaningful existence for Batman.

Dark Knight completes a structural inversion of the established

***The Dark Knight Returns*, page (a) 47. Two-Face as a reflection of Batman's divided personality.**

pattern of the superhero story. In the stories of the Golden Age, Silver Age and after, the superheroes enjoyed the backing of a social consensus – even if its terms and ideology were left undefined. There would be a preferred and arguably hegemonic reading of any particular superhero text. Villains intent on disrupting the consensus and overturning the social order were the protagonists of individual stories, while the superhero remained the protagonist of his overall myth.

Dark Knight takes the Batman myth out of this hegemonic consensus. However, it doesn't set Batman up as a subversive counter-myth. Batman is presented as a marginal figure, supported by some, attacked by others. Crucially, the supportive Commissioner Gordon is replaced by the hostile Yindel. Batman is reinstated as protagonist at the specific expense of continuity. The text can claim to be a genuine graphic novel – and not simply four shorter stories bound up into book form – chiefly because its central character undergoes a genuine process of character development. The Batman seen on the last page, organizing his underground army of ex-Mutants, is not the same person as the self-destructive Bruce Wayne we have been introduced to on page 1, all but killing himself to win a motor race. But Miller's achievement in *Dark Knight* begs the question: if the intention is to treat superheroes in a novelistic way breaking away from continuity, why not start with a completely clean slate? Such is Alan Moore and Dave Gibbons' *Watchmen*.

Watchmen

Quis custodiet ipsos Custodes?
(Who watches the Watchmen?)

Juvenal, *Satires*, VI, 347

Watchmen was published by DC Comics in 12 monthly instalments between October 1986 and September 1987. The entire series has since been reissued as a trade paperback, which is probably the best way to approach the text of *Watchmen* – as the graphic novel format strongly emphasizes the structured and unified character of the whole.

Watchmen is the story of a vigilante superhero (Rorschach) and his efforts to solve the mystery behind the death of a super-patriotic, right-wing superhero called the Comedian (aka Edward Blake). His investigation involves a number of other costumed characters and superheroes – Silk Spectre, Dr Manhattan, Ozymandias, Nite Owl – and takes place in 1985 in a New York which forms part of what science fiction writers call an 'alternative world': some things in the world of *Watchmen* are the same as our own, others are different. Differences include a President Nixon who has amended the US Constitution in order to remain in power for five consecutive terms, electrically propelled cars and airships, and a history of crime-fighting costumed vigilantes. Pretty much unchanged are the tension between the superpowers, and the inner-city crime and paranoia.

But the *mise en scène* of *Watchmen* is one in which the existence of a superpowered and seemingly omnipotent superhero (Dr Manhattan) has significantly upset the balance of terror. The USSR is helpless in the face of Dr Manhattan's powers, which have been used by a triumphant President Nixon to ensure victory for the US in the Vietnam War. The Soviet Union is sufficiently unnerved by the power of Dr Manhattan to be thought ready to initiate a pre-emptive nuclear strike, just to even up the odds. Furthermore, superheroes and vigilantes are unpopular with both the public and police, and have been outlawed since a police strike and subsequent anti-superhero rioting in 1977. Rorschach continues to operate outside the umbrella of the law, while Dr Manhattan and (until his death) the Comedian operate only with the official sanction of the US Government. Rorschach's investigations of the Blake murder eventually bring back into action Nite Owl, a gadget-oriented, Batman-style superhero, and Laurie Juszpeczyk (the Silk Spectre), a karate-kicking superheroine.

The reader comes to know the Comedian chiefly through flashback, mainly in *Watchmen* 1,2,4,6, and 9, as other characters reveal different sides of the Comedian's personality. The Comedian is ruthless, cynical and nihilistic, and yet capable of deeper insights than the others into the role of the costumed hero. He patriotically supports US involvement in Vietnam, and yet is entirely cynical about the motives behind the war:

> Average Vietnamese don't give a damn who won. It means something to the dinks and it means plenty to us . . .[29]

This remark is made just after the US has won. But when faced with a rioting crowd of New Yorkers, the Comedian laughs down Nite Owl's voice of liberal conscience:

> What's happened to America? What's happened to the American dream?
>
> It came true. You're lookin' at it. Now c'mon . . . Let's really put these jokers through some changes.[30]

The Comedian belongs firmly in the tradition of the existential men of action who come to realize themselves through violent conflict and death – such as William Holden in *The Wild Bunch* or Warren

Oates in *Bring Me The Head of Alfredo Garcia*. More than just tough guys, these heroes or anti-heroes follow through the logic of their code, even if it leads to their own destruction. A realistic rendering of the traditional superhero code would have meant the same fate for Batman many times over – imagine the Batman movie as Sam Peckinpah might have written and directed it, ending perhaps, as *The Wild Bunch* does, with the hero embracing his own death against overwhelming opposition.

The Comedian discovers by chance Adrian [Ozymandias] Veidt's plot to create an artificial alien menace to unite the superpowers and prevent nuclear war. The Comedian's resulting bloody defenestration kicks off the action of the plot as the investigation is taken up by Rorschach. Veidt is eventually discovered to be behind the superhero murders.

While the Comedian is in part a satirical reworking of the state-sponsored, nationalistic breed of superhero most notably exemplified by Captain America or Nick Fury, Rorschach is a version of the night-shrouded hero embodied by characters from Batman through Daredevil to the Question and the Punisher. Rorschach is a vigilante who preys on the fears of lawbreakers but is almost completely outside the bounds of the society he chooses to protect. Visiting Nite Owl (Dan Dreiberg) to give him news of the Comedian's death, Rorschach opens a can of beans and slurps them unheated into his mouth, half pulling up his mask to do so. Several characters complain of Rorschach's unpleasant body odour: he lives his alter-ego life in a tiny and filthy bedsit where he accuses his landlady of being a whore. By day he patrols the streets with a placard warning of the end of the world: questioning suspects at night involves breaking their fingers one by one until they talk. Rorschach's latex mask is made from material taken from a dress ordered from the factory where he worked after leaving the orphanage in which he grew up. The girl who ordered the dress was subsequently murdered in a sexual assault: the murder fuels Rorschach's resolve to clean up society. Rorschach, in short, is cut from the template of the vigilante superhero, but with every semblance of glamour apparently taken away.[31]

Nite Owl and Silk Spectre have already been discussed in chapter two, which leaves – of the major characters in *Watchmen* – the two visions of the superhero as a Nietzschean Superman: Doctor Manhattan and Ozymandias. Each has arrived at their superior status by very different routes: Doctor Manhattan via an accident in a nuclear physics laboratory, and Ozymandias through a concerted development of the mental and physical powers latent in every individual. Doctor Manhattan's accidental omnipotence leads him further and further away from human concerns; Ozymandias's lesser but deliberately sought powers bring with them a desire to control and reform human affairs from above through direct intervention.

Watchmen is a complex and multi-faceted text which employs a number of self-consciously 'post-modernist' literary strategies, to emphasize its status as (among other things) a fairly systematic critique of the development of the superhero genre in sequential art. The most immediately striking of these strategies is the use made of the last four pages of each issue – space often given over in comics to a letters page or announcements of forthcoming titles, such as the long-running 'Stan's Soapbox' in Marvel's titles. Moore and Gibbons make use of these pages in each issue of *Watchmen* to present a text essay or collage of text materials relating to the theme and background of that issue or the developing storyline as a whole.

Watchmen 1–3 fills in the background of superhero development from 1939 onwards, via excerpts from ex-superhero Hollis Mason's autobiography *Under The Hood*. Mason, now retired, had been the original Nite Owl. These first three 'autobiographical' inserts fill in much of the background to *Watchmen* – especially the development of the costumed characters and their relationship to the alterative history being presented of the 1939–1985 period.

As we have seen, origin stories are a key part of superhero continuity, places where the motivation behind a character's heroism can be elaborated or even reinvented as the series develops. Watchmen's once-off characters need to be explained within the context of a single unfolding story. Several of the characters in *Under the Hood* had been authority figures before they turned to the life of masked vigilante – soldiers or cops. The wave of heroes active in *Watchmen's* 1940s, the Golden Age equivalent, are integrated into American society and foreign policy in telling ways. Dollar Bill – a Captain America look-alike – is a hero sponsored by one of the largest US banks. The bank insists that Dollar Bill wear a costume designed for maximum publicity exposure, and featuring a cape:

> While attempting to stop a raid upon one of his employer's banks, his cloak became entangled in the bank's revolving doors and he was shot dead at point blank range before he could free it. Designers employed by the bank had designed his costume for maximum publicity appeal. If he'd designed it himself he might have left out that damned stupid cloak and still be alive today.[32]

The superheroes exist at the mercy of contingent factors, which limit their actions – whether by forcing them to wear impractical costumes or by the passing of anti-vigilante legislation. Far from representing a fantasy of power, the superhero in *Watchmen* has become just another facet of society, and is consequently debunked. Satire replaces explicit mythology.

The fake excerpts from texts placed at the conclusion of each chapter of *Watchmen* focus in turn on the key characters and themes of the story. After Hollis Mason's background pieces in 1–3, the spotlight turns to Dr Manhattan in 4, pirate comics in 5, Rorschach in 6, an essay on ornithology by Daniel (Nite Owl) Dreiberg in 7, an issue of the far-right newsletter the *New Frontiersman* in 8, a collection of biographical fragments concerning the first Silk Spectre, Laurie Juspeczyk's mother in 9, a collection of documents relating to Adrian (Ozymandias) Veidt in 10 and 'After The Masquerade', an interview with Veidt by Gonzo-style journalist Doug Roth from the left-leaning weekly *Nova Express*. Episode 12 concludes the story and contains no textual tailpiece: it uses the equivalent space for a four-page splash of the destruction of Manhattan by Adrian Veidt's faked alien invasion.

Clearly, all this multi-textual apparatus is an open invitation to readers to provide their own context for the story. Moore deliberately invites the reader to engage in a self-conscious reading of the graphic novel text, one which involves accommodating that part of the text (the tailpieces) which are tricked up to appear as 'commentary' on the main text. All this assumes that the reader is very literate in comic-books, and fully conversant with the subculture in which the superhero comics exist. One example of this is the characterization of Veidt as purveyor of the 'Veidt Method' of self-realization. This can only be fully appreciated if the reader is familiar with the body-building courses and home education schemes found on the advertising pages of monthly comic-books. ('What if I'm laid off? Will automation take my job? . . . Will my job ever pay more? BE A SKILLED LOCKSMITH'). Veidt adopts exactly this tone of voice to promote his 'method'.

> Hello. If you're reading this, it's because you sent away for my course, and if you did THAT, it's because you think you need a change in your life. A better body? Increased confidence and magnetism? Advanced mental techniques that will help you at home and in business? Well, yes, we can offer you all these things . . . but in order to have and enjoy them, there's got to be a new YOU![33]

This is one of the many ways in which Moore and Gibbons subvert the expectations of the reader. If Veidt (ultimately revealed as *Watchmen's* 'villain') purveys the same self-improvement schemes as can be found in the advertising pages of comics, then the typical superhero reader becomes one of the subjects of *Watchmen's* discourse. The negative or limiting values placed on superheroes by the expectations of fans (or the interpretation of those demands, as understood by editors and writers) are all the subject of critical commentary through the persona of Veidt, who retires from his role as superhero because he sees more potential to help the world through business:

> I guess I've just reached a point where I'm starting to wonder whether all the grandstanding and fighting individual evils does much good for the world as a whole . . . Maybe as a businessman I can do more good, on a more meaningful scale.[34]

And it is Veidt's plan to 'help the world' which forms the spine of *Watchmen's* plot. Veidt kidnaps artists and comic creators to fabricate artificial aliens that are teleported into the centre of Manhattan, initiating a fake 'menace' from space that defuses superpower tension and averts a nuclear showdown. Instead of reacting to individual menaces to society, he takes the initiative. As we have seen in chapter two, this is normally the role of the villain and, sure enough, Veidt does become Watchmen's 'villain'. The Comedian, nominally still a 'hero', has become equally ruthless in his defence of the status quo.

Chapters 3,5,8,9,10 and 11 of *Watchmen* feature the device of a comic-within-a-comic. This is the 'pirate comic' story 'Marooned', supposedly taken from issues 23–24 of *The Black Freighter*, presented as having been published in the early 1960s, as part of an invented boom in comics featuring pirate-oriented material. Not content with rewriting the history of the post-war era, Moore is here reworking the history of the comic-book itself.[35] Parts of the text of 'Marooned' are inserted into *Watchmen* through the device of a young black New Yorker seen reading a *Black Freighter* comic. The story is also summarized in the non-graphic text section at the end of *Watchmen* 5, as part of an excerpt from a bogus history of comic books. The story concerns

> . . . a young mariner whose vessel is wrecked by the Black Freighter before it can return to its hometown and warn of the hell-ship's approach. Cast adrift on an uninhabited island with only his dead shipmates for company, we experience the frantic mariner's torment at the knowledge that while he is trapped on the island, the bestial crew of the Freighter are surely bearing down upon his town, his home, his wife and his children. Driven by his burning desire to avert this calamity, we see the mariner finally escape from the island by what may be one of the most striking and dramatic devices thus far in pirate comic books: digging up the gas-bloated corpses of his shipmates, the mariner lashes them together and uses them as floats on an improvised raft on which he hopes to reach the mainland . . . On reaching the mainland safely upon his horrific craft we see the increasingly dis-

> traught and dishevelled mariner trying desperately to reach his home, even resorting to murder to acquire a horse for himself.[36]

The textual summary becomes less precise from here on. It is appended to *Watchmen* 5, and the *Black Freighter* story doesn't reach its conclusion until 11. On arrival in his home port of Davidstown, the mariner believes the town to be under the occupation of the crew of the Freighter. He steals secretly into his own home, expecting to surprise members of the Freighter's crew busy pillaging and raping his family. The mariner strikes out in the darkened bedroom at a moving figure, only to realize too late that he has murdered his own wife. There is nothing left but to return to the seashore, where the hell-ship is waiting for him. He swims out to it and is hauled aboard.

The mariner is forced by the urgency of his vengeance mission to shed one inhibition after another: using the bloated bodies of his comrades as floats, killing the first man he meets on the mainland and stealing his horse, and finally enacting the violence against innocents feared from the crew of the *Black Freighter*, thus carrying out the carnage he had striven to prevent. Just like Ozymandias/Adrian Veidt, he hopes to stave off disaster by using the dead bodies of his former comrades as a means of reaching his goal.

In contrast to the almost silent concentration of the youth reading the *Black Freighter* comic, the newsagent himself is garrulous to a fault. He's always ready to offer his opinions on the news and world affairs, such as the looming threat of nuclear war:

> We oughta nuke Russia, and let God sort it out. I mean, I read the signs, read the headlines, look things inna face, y'know? I'm a newsvendor, Goddamit! I'm informed on the situation! We oughta nuke 'em till they glow! Course, that's just my opinion.[37]

Laid over the same panels, but lettered in a scroll-style with the corners turned up, are narrative panels giving the opening words of the *Black Freighter* story:

> Delerious, I saw that hell-bound ship's black sails against the yellow Indies sky, and knew again the stench of powder, and men's brains, and war . . .
>
> Its tar-streaked hull rolled over me. In despair I sank beneath those foul, pink billows, offering up my wretched soul to almighty God, his mercy and his judgement.[38]

The accompanying panels execute the graphic novel's equivalent to a cinematic 'pull back to reveal'. Panel one is filled with a close-up of a black symbol, difficult to decipher. It could be the black sails of the *Black Freighter*. The next panel reveals this yellow-over-black

FOR WHAT THAT'S WORTH, Y'KNOW?
INNA FINAL ANALYSIS.
WAKING FROM NIGHTMARE, I FOUND MYSELF UPON A DISMAL BEACH-HEAD, AMONGST DEAD MEN AND THE PIECES OF DEAD MEN.
LISSEN, I SEE EVERY GODDAMN FRONT PAGE INNA WORLD. I ABSORB INFORMATION! I MISS NOTHING.
BOSUN RIDLEY LAY NEARBY. BIRDS WERE EATING HIS THOUGHTS AND MEMORIES.
FR'INSTANCE ...THE MORE DISASTERS HAPPEN, THE MORE PAPERS I SELL! EXPLAIN THAT!
READER, TAKE COMFORT FROM THIS: IN HELL, AT LEAST THE GULLS ARE CONTENTED.
SEE, EVERYTHING'S CONNECTED. A NEWSVENDOR UNNERSTANDS THAT. HE DON'T RETREAT FROM REALITY.
FOR MY PART, I BEGGED THAT THEY SHOULD TAKE MY EYES, THUS SPARING ME FURTHER HORRORS.
UNHEEDED, I STOOD IN THE SURF AND WEPT, UNABLE TO BEAR MY CIRCUMSTANCES.
THE WEIGHT O' THE WORLD'S ON HIM, BUT DOES HE QUIT? NAH! HE'S LIKE ATLAS! HE CAN TAKE IT!
HE'S A SURVIVOR.
IT'S LIKE THIS AFTERNOON: NOVA EXPRESS IS HOLDIN' ITS FRONT PAGE, SO NO DELIVERY 'TIL TONIGHT. A CATASTROPHE!
...BUT I COPED!
EVENTUALLY, TEARS CEASED. MY MISFORTUNES WERE SMALL: I WAS ALIVE...
NEWSVENDORS ALWAYS COPE! THEY'RE INDESTRUCTIBLE! THEY THRIVE ON DISASTER! THEY...
...AND I KNEW THAT LIFE HAD NO WORSE NEWS TO OFFER ME.
OH. GOOD AFTERNOON, SIR.
THE END IS NIGH
GOOD AFTERNOON.
IS IT HERE YET?

shape for what it is: part of a fallout shelter sign – thus linking the mariner's nemesis of the *Black Freighter* with Adrian Veidt's desire to avert nuclear war. And panel three places this in the context of a street – and simultaneously slips in references to the 'missing writer' subplot, by way of a pinned up cover of the *New Frontiersman*. Panel four – a large one, covering the remaining two-thirds of the page – sets all this in context: the news stand, the street, the man tacking up fallout shelter signs. The first six panels of the next page, which return to a regular nine panels to a page format, complete the movement with a 'zooming in' effect – starting from the opposite side of the street and closing in on the open page of the *Black Freighter* comic. Text is a mixture of speech balloons and more 'scrolled' panels from the *Black Freighter* subplot.

The three panels which form the middle tier of the page use the emerging figure of the mariner to comment on the soliloquy of the newsvendor. The left-hand panel shows the youth holding the comic book, but shadowed, so that the light falls strongly only on the page of the comic. The speech balloon from the off-stage newsvendor is placed alongside the 'scrolled' narrative panel from the *Black Freighter* story, which resembles small panels which can be seen inside the open comic it is 'taken from'. The open page of the *Black Freighter* comic itself shows three panels: a large splash panel of the mariner standing in the surf surrounded by wreckage, and two smaller ones. One of these shows him with his head in his hands, the third is largely obscured by the youth's hand and cigarette.

The central panel focuses wholly on the pirate comic book: we can see nothing that lies outside its pages. The top panel glimpsed in the previous panel is now all that we see, and it is rendered in full colour, making it, in effect, a typical *Watchmen* panel in its size, shape, and density of detail. Again, two narrative panels are juxtaposed against the image of the lone surviving mariner: the 'scrolled text' from the *Black Freighter* story:

> Unheeded, I stood in the surf and wept, unable to bear my circumstances.[39]

and the speech balloon of the newsvendor, ruminating on the strengths of his own kind:

> The weight o' the world's on him, but does he quit? Nah! He's like Atlas! He can take it![40]

The right-hand panel completes this 'zoom' on the open page of the

***Watchmen* 3, page 2. The introduction of the Black Freighter subplot.**

Black Freighter comic book. But whilst the panel on the left shows a comic book drawn within a comic book, and the central panel a panel from that comic rendered in the style of the surrounding material, the panel on the right has gone in too close for comfort; the limitations of the panel (the part we can still see) have started to become apparent. All that remain visible are the mariner's head and a fragment of flat yellow and blue, identifiable as sea and sand from the previous panel, but abstract if taken on their own. The bottom half of the panel is filled with the mariner's head – the same head depicted previously.

But it doesn't look like that. The right-hand panel simulates the effect of a comic-book seen from too-close. The mariner's face, distraught enough in the previous panel, has become a nightmare mask of despair: blank, drained of humanity, crude in execution. Its garish horrors are oversized and laid bare. Over the staring face of the mariner, at the top of the panel, Moore has laid the final speech balloon from the vendor's soliloquy:

> He's a survivor.[41]

At one level, this completes the praise of the stoicism of newsvendors ('He's like Atlas! He can take it! He's a survivor'.) But the whole sequence of panels has been building towards laying these words against the image of the marooned sailor, plucked out of scale and context ('See, everything's connected. A newsvendor understands that. He don't retreat from reality').

This is an example of sequential art at its very best, but it also sheds light on Moore and Gibbons's deepest intentions. *Watchmen* is at bottom about the inventions and fictions employed by everybody either to achieve power and control or simply to get through their daily lives. The youth reading the *Black Freighter* comic fails to grasp the significance of the story before he is obliterated in Adrian Veidt's attack on New York – an event which, for the alert reader of *Watchmen*, is echoed by the story of the marooned mariner. There are no privileged cases: superheroes, presidents, psychiatrists, newsvendors, journalists, admen; all are presented as consumers of their own self-serving fictions. And, presumably, readers of superhero comics as well – burying their heads in a story they don't understand while the world falls around their ears.

Thus *Watchmen* builds up a world which is both morally ambiguous and full of semiological complexity – a far cry from the clear-cut semiotics of Siegel and Shuster's *Superman*. Into this awkward and puzzling environment are introduced several competing versions of the costumed hero: Rorshach, The Comedian, Nite Owl, Silk Spectre, Dr Manhattan, Ozymandias. In a once-off text, they have none of the mechanisms of continuity to give automatic resonance to their roles. In a flashback to the 1960s, Captain Metropolis – a superhero left over from the forties – attempts to band the existing heroes into a crimefighting team:

> Well, as you know, this country hasn't had an organization of masked adventurers since the Minutemen disbanded in '49.
> Specialized law enforcement is standing still. Crime isn't. New social evils emerge every day: promiscuity, drugs, campus subversion, you name it! Now, by banding together as the Crimebusters, we . . .[42]

But the Comedian's response is 'Bullshit . . . you're gettin' old and you want to go on playin' Cowboys and Indians.' Ozymandias steps in to support the idea of the Crimebusters team:

> It doesn't require genius to see that America has problems that need tackling . . .[43]

And the Comedian responds

> Damn straight. And it takes a moron to think they're small enough for clowns like you guys to handle. What's going down in this world, you got no idea. Believe me.[44]

The superhero declares his own irrelevance, which clears the way for the Comedian to engage in a nihilistic and cynical career of mercenary violence. Furthermore, the superheroes in *Watchmen* fail to congeal into a team. The differences between them are too great – differences in powers, differences in moral and political temperament. Such contrasts between heroes are normally glossed over by the smoothing and healing effects of continuity: in the continuity team comic, differences between heroes exist (such as the problems between the Falcon and the Avengers), but all converge within the same overarching myth. While *The Avengers* relishes teaming Norse God Thor with the human Captain America, *Watchmen* continually stresses the oddness of classing normal and superpowered heroes together. The normal conventions of continuity are deliberately undercut. In *Watchmen* 4 Dr Manhattan attends '. . . a charity event with several costumed adventurers attending . . . friendly middle-aged men who like to dress up. I have nothing in common with them.' The Comedian is equally dubious about Dr Manhattan: 'You're driftin' outta touch, Doc. You're turnin' into a flake. God help us all.'

As well as lacking the underpinning structure of continuity, the superheroes of *Watchmen* also lack any supervillains to measure themselves against. They are forced to confront more intangible moral and social concerns. The superhero is removed from all the normal narrative expectations of the genre. *Dark Knight* handles

WHY "THE CRIME-BUSTERS"?
WELL, AS YOU KNOW, THIS COUNTRY HASN'T HAD AN ORGANIZATION OF MASKED ADVENTURERS SINCE THE MINUTEMEN DISBANDED IN '49.

SPECIALIZED LAW ENFORCEMENT IS STANDING STILL. CRIME ISN'T.
NEW SOCIAL EVILS EMERGE EVERY DAY: PROMISCUITY, DRUGS, CAMPUS SUBVERSION, YOU NAME IT! NOW, BY BANDING TOGETHER AS THE CRIME-BUSTERS, WE...
BULLSHIT.

WHAT?
I SAID BULLSHIT. THIS WHOLE IDEA, THIS CRIMEBUSTERS SHTICK, IT STINKS.
WHAT IT IS, NELLY, IS THAT YOU'RE GETTIN' OLD AND YOU WANNA GO ON PLAYIN' COWBOYS AND INDIANS!

TH-THAT ISN'T TRUE...
UH, LISTEN, LET'S NOT THROW THE IDEA OUT RIGHT AWAY. ME AND RORSCHACH HAVE MADE HEADWAY INTO THE GANGS PROBLEM BY POOLING OUR EFFORTS...

OBVIOUSLY, I AGREE -- BUT A GROUP THIS SIZE SEEMS MORE LIKE A PUBLICITY EXERCISE SOMEHOW. IT'S TOO BIG AND UNWIELDY...
SURELY, THAT'S JUST AN ORGANIZATIONAL PROBLEM? WITH THE RIGHT PERSON COORDINATING THE GROUP, I THINK...

OH, AN' I WONDER WHO THAT WOULD BE?
GOT ANY IDEAS, OZZY? I MEAN, YOU ARE THE SMARTEST GUY IN THE WORLD, RIGHT?
IT DOESN'T REQUIRE GENIUS TO SEE THAT AMERICA HAS PROBLEMS THAT NEED TACKLING.

DAMN STRAIGHT. AN' IT TAKES A MORON TO THINK THEY'RE SMALL ENOUGH FOR CLOWNS LIKE YOU GUYS TO HANDLE.
WHAT'S GOING DOWN IN THIS WORLD, YOU GOT NO IDEA.
BELIEVE ME.

this theme through the inversion of an established hero: *Watchmen* does it by creating heroes outside their familiar context. Miller's Batman succeeds in re-modelling a miniature society in his own image – by going underground into the sewers. Moore's Veidt achieves his objective of avoiding nuclear conflict – at the cost of three million dead in New York from his faked extra-terrestrial attack.

Watchmen's so-called 'postmodernism' largely comprises this process of stripping away the accumulation of 50 years of continuity. In so doing, Moore and Gibbons have produced a text which transcends the accumulated myths through which superhero texts are read – they have, so to speak, stretched the boundaries of the genre. (Nevertheless, *Watchmen* does conform to all seven definitions of the superhero story set out in chapter one). The extent of the text's ironic self awareness of the genre's history, and the technique by which stock superhero types such as Nite Owl and The Comedian are interrogated to the point where their mythology collapses into new levels of literal meaning, all mark out *Watchmen* either as the last key superhero text, or the first in a new maturity of the genre.

Although *Watchmen* and *Dark Knight* may have opened doors to new approaches in superhero comics, it ought to be pointed out that Alan Moore has frequently spoken of *Watchmen* and his subsequent Batman story *The Killing Joke* as an end, rather than a new beginning. He is less than happy about the influence of his own and Frank Miller's work:

> . . . obviously, we've to some degree doomed the mainstream comics medium to a parade of violent, depressing postmodern superheroes, a lot of whom, in addition to those other faults, are incredibly pretentious. I stand accused.[45]

In particular, Moore is unhappy about the reception of Rorshach, the key character and moral barometer of the story.

> If you're a vigilante then this is what you're going to be like: you're not going to have any friends because you're going to be crazy and obsessive and dangerous and frightening; you're probably going to be too obsessed with your vendetta to bother about things like eating or washing or tidying your room because what have they got to do with the War Against Crime? . . .
>
> Undoubtedly, at the end of the day – whatever else *Watchmen* did – the most popular character in it was Rorschach. And I really don't think that he was a popular character because of his ironic portrayal

***Watchmen* 2, page 10. No place for the superhero?**

> of the worthlessness of the vigilante ideal. I think people were getting off on him because he was a tough, scary, frightening character that they identified with.[46]

The genre's limitations seem to lie within the expectations of the audience. These remarks were published in 1990, two years after Moore wrote his last superhero graphic novel, *The Killing Joke* – which is really a story about the Joker in which Batman plays a major but secondary role. Since then, Moore has abandoned any attempt to comment on the superhero genre from the inside, and has turned to graphic novels such as the unfinished *Big Numbers* and *A Small Killing*, which deal in similar themes to Moore's superhero stories, but through the post-modernist use of soap-opera and thriller conventions. In fact, a move in this direction was visible even in *Watchmen*, with the foregrounding of several non-costumed characters who play key roles in the narrative – such as Rorschach's psychiatrist Dr Malcolm Long.

It may well be (as many critics are now arguing) that the superhero genre belongs to the early days of the comic. The rules of continuity and the audience's expectations may mean that nothing further can be achieved. If that is the case – if the development of comics carries their momentum away from the superhero – it will be telling to observe what becomes of the key superheroes and their myths. It is even possible that, released from the treadmill of monthly serial continuity, one or two of the most effective superhero myths might ascend the cultural ladder and become established as suitable vehicles for 'high art'. One could argue that, since more people now know Superman and Batman through the movies than through their regular comics, this process is already underway.

EPILOGUE

In a story beginning in *Superman* 74, dated December 1992, the Man of Steel teams up with the Justice League to fight a new menace dubbed 'Doomsday'. Doomsday is eight or nine feet tall, covered from head to foot in a dark green boiler suit, and so savage and powerful that he overwhelms the combined strength of the Justice League, leaving several members close to death. Superman embarks on a desperate defensive struggle with Doomsday—at first in partnership with the Justice League and then on his own. Doomsday continues his destructive progress from somewhere in Ohio (where he first emerges from what seems to be an underground prison) to Metropolis.

In his path, Doomsday leaves scores of innocent bystanders killed or injured. His green boiler suit is ripped away piece by piece, revealing a dark grey body of Incredible Hulk-like proportions, accentuated as even more menacing by sharp bony protruberances at the knuckles, elbows, shoulders, face and knees. Doomsday acts without visible plan or motivation, beyond a barely-vocalized intent to reach Metropolis—partly fuelled (in one of the story's more droll moments) by a video promotion for a WFA wrestling extravaganza.

Superman is determined to 'hold the line' in Metropolis. Costume ripped and body bleeding, he is forced to withdraw from the battle to rescue a helicopter carrying Lois Lane and Jimmy Olsen: the duo have been reporting on the battle but have become caught up in it. ('The whole country will want to see Superman kick this creep's butt' says Lois's colleague Cat from a second helicopter.) In a moment's lull, Lois (now Superman's fiancée and aware of his dual identity as Clark Kent) urges caution:

> Maybe you should retreat and get help!
> If Jimmy is right . . .
>
> Too late, Lois. The JLA has already fallen and there are too many innocents in jeopardy right now! It's up to me.

With an unprecedented look of fury on his face, Superman goes back into battle. Once again, Lois and Jimmy become caught up in the fray, Lois momentarily offering herself as a decoy while Superman recovers his strength. 'Who is he? What does he want?' asks Lois. 'He wants destruction and death' answers Superman. 'To stop him I have to be every bit as ferocious and unrelenting as he is.' Like the nameless dragon which Beowulf fights after defeating Grendel and Grendel's mother, Doomsday's anonymity may be a key to the nature of the menace he is intended to embody.

The crisis of the battle is reached, and Superman makes a classic 'extra effort' speech:

> Exhausted . . . But I have to keep fighting until I drop . . . or he does . . . This is it! Looks like we're both betting everything we've got on this one! For Lois . . . and Jimmy . . . For this entire city . . . I've got to put this guy away while I still can!

So far, so normal. The superhero steels himself to make the extra effort that goes beyond what can normally be achieved. Superman even adduces totems of normality as the motivation for his battle: Lois, Jimmy, Metropolis. Both Superman and Doomsday unleash one final, explosive blow, and we turn the page expecting to see Superman tested to the very limit of his strength and emerging once again triumphant . . .

. . . except that the end of this particular battle is different. Lois cradles Superman in her arms. He asks her what happened: Lois tells him that Doomsday has been destroyed. And, turning over the back flap of the comic to reach the final, hidden panel, we see Superman collapsed and clearly dead—a point which the panel's caption reinforces with the words 'For this is a day . . . that a Superman dies.'

The 'Death of Superman' plotline climaxed at the end of 1992, a fitting conclusion to a year which had already witnessed notable events within both superhero continuity and subculture. The year had opened with a flurry of media interest in *Alpha Flight* 106, a title featuring Marvel's hitherto unremarkable *X-Men* spinoff Canadian superheroes. The cause of the sudden media interest was a story dealing with the theme of AIDS and the proclamation of a gay sexual orientation by Northstar, one of Alpha Flight's founder members.

Interestingly, much of the mainstream press coverage assumed that *Alpha Flight* was a new comic and Northstar a new superhero. In fact, the character and team had been around since 1979. Such coverage largely focussed on whether the subject of HIV and/or the gay superhero was a suitable one for a comic 'aimed at children' to explore. Some of the more sophisticated media coverage tried to draw parallels with the superhero's 'coming of age' in *Dark Knight*, *Watchmen* and the rest. The comparison was, however, a bogus one: *Alpha Flight* 106 is rooted firmly in the liberal conservatism of Stan Lee's Marvel comics, advocating passive support for those afflicted with the HIV virus in the same way that Lee's work on the 1960s *Daredevil*, *Silver Surfer* and other titles elicited sympathy for victims of racial or other prejudice. Alpha Flight's heroism enables the team to square up to the HIV virus much as they would to any other menace—only less effectively. *Alpha Flight* 106 commits the error of subjecting today's moral issues to yesterday's rhetoric. The comic had few defenders.

Of more lasting resonance within comic fandom was the continuing presence of new publishers determined to emulate, albeit on a smaller scale, the linked superhero continuities of the two premier publishers. *Archer and Armstrong*—published by newcomer Valiant comics—established itself as one of the few superhero titles still popular with the critics and fans alike. Valiant had been launched by ex-Marvel chief editor Jim Shooter: in 1993 Shooter left Valiant to set up yet another new company, Defiant. As with Valiant, Shooter's intention was to build an all-new DC/Marvel style continuity from the ground up.

Most notable of these new competitors to DC/Marvel supremacy was Image, who by 1993 were presenting a serious commercial challenge to both the older companies through their growing line of superhero comics such as *Spawn*, *Wildcats* and *Youngblood*. All these titles took the superhero genre to the borders of the horror/fantasy market, but during 1993 the company introduced its '1963' series, a bogus continuity set back in the heyday of the Silver Age and featuring ironic pastiches of the Fantastic Four, Iron Man, Spider Man and other familiar Marvel characters. Image even attracted Alan Moore and Dave Gibbons back into the superhero genre to work on the 1963 series. Moore continued to wrong-foot fans and critics alike by prolonging his connection with Image and writing an issue of *Spawn*, a comic which—in certain circles—had become synonymous with the remorseless violence of the contemporary superhero story. Despite—or perhaps because of—this bad publicity, celebrated artists and writers such as Frank Miller and Dave Sim seized the opportunity to work on the title.

Indeed, vilification of the superhero genre (and its readership) has become increasingly the stock-in-trade of a large section of the critical press. The following excerpt is from a letter published in *The Comics Journal* in 1993:

> . . . . Morons and children read 'normal' superhero comics. Adults with taste and a sense of humour (like myself, of course) read alternative comics. The two types of comics have nothing at all to do with each other, and in fact, may as well be sold in different stores.

Such views are regularly advanced by those who wish to 'get comics taken more seriously'. The anti-superhero stance can at times be almost reminiscent of the strictures of Fredric Wertham back in the fifties—only this time, the attack comes from within the caucus of comic fandom itself.

In the fifties, the moral and mental corruption of the horror or superhero comic was contrasted with the spiritual uplift of theatre and the novel—at a time when, ironically, the absurdism of Beckett or Ionesco and the head-trips of William Burroughs comprised the cutting edge of European and American literature. Nowadays, 'alternative' or 'adult' comics (having more-or-less caught up with the post-war intellectual mainstream) are used as a stick to beat the superhero and other forms of genre writing. The comics hierarchy is thus restructuring itself as a diminutive reflection of the mainstream culture which still largely rejects it.

Arguably, what is currently occurring is a stage in the evolution of American comics as a whole into an auteur-dominated medium. The kind of collaboration—sometimes anonymous, usually underpaid which produced the superhero comics of the forties, fifties and sixties has given way to the elevation of autonomous individual expression. Dave Sim, writer/illustrator/publisher of the renowned *Cerebus the Aardvark*, is an incisive proponent of this view:

> You might be curious as to why this column is called 'Note from the President'. It is partly a play on the fact that I am the president of Aardvark Vanaheim; the publishing company which I own and which published the reprint volumes and the monthly comic book. But it also has a great deal to do with my particular perception of the ideal role for the comic book creator; to preside over his creativity. Nothing is done with Cerebus as a character, a comic book, a story-line or a commercial entity without my express approval. I don't have a 'boss' who tells me how things are or are not going to go. As a reader, whether you love what I'm doing here, or whether you hate it, you only have one person to point your finger at.

Nothing could be further from the fate of Siegel and Shuster, signing away their rights to Superman. Nothing could be further from the linked creative endeavours of continuity-based superhero stories. And nothing could be further from the current Superman comics: four separate monthly titles employing separate writer/artist teams to produce a single storyline in continuity. And yet it is within this tight, weekly continuity that Superman died and returned to life as four separate entities.

Arguably, the death/rebirth Superman plot is the most complete demonstration so far of the superhero story as an evolving mythology. The most famous superhero of all has been killed off, only to come back as four disconnected fragments, a fractured prism through which the reader perceives distorted images of the original. These four characters were: a black construction worker/scientist in a steel suit, a punk Superboy sporting a black leather jacket, a cyborg with half of

Superman's face, and an authoritarian Kryptonian who looks like Clark Kent but acts without Superman's compassion for humanity.

Each creative team focused on the adventures of one of the Supermen, as the plotline worked towards resolving which, if any, of these was the real McCoy. But, paradoxically, by splitting the Superman myth into its component parts, the primacy of the original is strengthened. All other Supermen are partial refractions of the original, a myth which no longer walks the Earth in visible flesh. Yet the narrative vitality of these partial Supermen is dependent on their ability to excite a subjective connection with the unchanging original, in which the reader's imagination has invested so much energy. Each of these fragmentary Supermen embody elements of the superhero myth as it is currently conceived: the alien; the inhuman, the adolescent, the outsider. The four reborn Supermen—fighting amongst themselves to prove their authenticity—provide a neat visual metaphor for the contemporary deconstruction of the Superhero into warring components.

It would be easy to suggest a link between this deconstruction of Superman himself, and the perceived erosion of the social and political structures represented by Superman's own particular version of the American Dream. But the symbolism can function just as happily outside the United States. In place of a mythologized perfect being, embodying strength, intelligence, wisdom, compassion, loyalty and courage, we read of fragmented virtues and signs, operating in isolation, but drawing such significance as they can from their common origin and shared cultural roots. This is a familiar discourse in contemporary culture. An artist such as Madonna can similarly draw on the widely dispersed power of Christian symbolism in order to capture her audience's imagination and simultaneously confound their expectations.

But, nevertheless, it has to be accepted that the death and rebirth of Superman as actually published by DC sits a little uncomfortably with the weight of symbolism granted it in the previous paragraph. Nothing has quite the resonance that it could. Perhaps one clue to explaining this lies in the state of Superman's continuity immediately prior to the battle with Doomsday.

The Superman who is killed in *Superman* 75 is not the same character who is discussed in chapter one of this book. Continuity had been broken and revamped from the ground up during the 'Crisis On Infinite Earths' story of 1985-86. And the Superman of the new continuity had started to evolve in a somewhat different manner—most notably when (to the consternation of the media) the Man of Steel revealed his Clark Kent identity to Lois Lane, who became his fiancée. These are not the actions of a static icon of adolescence, but of an evolving individual moving towards marriage, maturity and fatherhood—something like the 'retired' Jordan Elliott of the Alan Moore story 'Whatever Happened to the Man of Tomorrow?'

To kill an individual in the process of self-discovery is the stuff of tragedy, and Superman's death in *Superman* 75, a weeping Lois cradling him in imitation of the Pieta, alludes to the Christian world's most familiar tragic model. The tendency in John Byrne's post-Crisis Superman was very much in this direction: to depict a character more 'human', more accessible, and more capable of recognizable emotional development. Marriage to Lois would have been one possible and logical outcome to such a storyline, and could have resulted in a retirement 'end of Superman' plotline of great interest and resonance. Instead, we are offered the blank destructive anonymity of Doomsday, a villain so radically lacking in personality and characterization that the reader is forced to infer that some representation of the caprice and absurdity of fate is the writer's intention.

Sherlock Holmes came back after his death at the hands of Professor Moriarty—but, as attentive readers observed, he was never quite the same man. In killing Superman and bringing him back in alternative forms, DC's four teams of writers and artists have—consciously or not—produced an ironic commentary on the crisis which the traditional superhero story is experiencing. The four separate creative teams, yoked into uneasy unity, exemplify the uncomfortable truce between the demands of continuity and the demands of auteurist self-expression. And the diversified Supermen—embodying an amalgam of influences from Cyberpunk to the Punisher to New Kids on the Block—awkwardly but effectively express conflicting trends within the superhero genre as a whole. Trends that are finding expression in a similar 'deconstruction' of Batman, in progress even as I write.

These conflicts will remain, even when the original Superman is stuck together from the fragments.

SELECT LIST OF FURTHER READING

Critical and Historical Background

Barker, Martin, *Comics: Ideology, power & the critics*, Manchester University Press, 1989. An all-round critical survey of the field, though superhero comics are not Barker's chief concern here.

Barrier, Michael and Williams, Martin, *A Smithsonian Book of Comic-Book Comics*, Smithsonian Institution Press/Harry N. Abrahams Inc., 1981. Excellent historical introduction, several classic reprints from the Golden Age.

Benton, Mike, *The Comic Book in America: An Illustrated History*, Taylor Publishing Company, 1989. A perceptive general history, well illustrated.

Browne, Ray B., Fishwick, Marshall and Marsden, Michael T., *Heroes of Popular Culture*, Bowling Green University Popular Press, 1972. The essays on Babe Ruth and Perry Mason are particularly illuminating.

Campbell, Joseph, *The Hero With a Thousand Faces*, Second Edition, Bollingen, 1968. Classic work of comparative mythology, with numerous points of application to superhero myths.

The Comics Journal, ed. Gary Groth. An outstanding source of critical writing on comics and much else besides.

Dooley, Dennis and Engle, Gary, *Superman at Fifty! The Persistence of a Legend*!, Octavia Press, 1987. Excellent collection of essays on Superman.

Feiffer, Jules, *The Great Comic Book Heroes*, The Dial Press, 1965. Light on text, but strong on Golden Age reprints.

Fresnoult-Deruelle, Piere, *La Bande Dessinee*, Hochette, 1972. Seminal structuralist analysis of the comic book.

Gifford, Denis, *The International Book of Comics*, Crescent Books, 1984. A visual introduction to the overall history of the comic-book.

Goulart, Ron, *Ron Goulart's Great History of Comic Books*, Contemporary Books, 1986. Goulart is best on the detailed history of the Golden Age.

Groth, Gary and Fiore, Robert, *The New Comics*, Berkley, 1988. Collection of interviews taken from the Comics Journal: includes Frank Miller, Alan Moore and Dave Gibbons.

Inge, M Thomas, *Comics as Culture*, University Press of Mississippi, 1990. Excellent collection of studies ranging over the whole field.

Kane, Bob, *Batman & Me*, Eclipse Books, 1989. Egocentric but entertaining insight into Batman's creator. Contains Golden Age Batman material in reprint.

Overstreet, Robert M., *The Overstreet Comic Book Price Guide*, Avon Books, 22nd Edition, 1992. The collector's bible.

Pearson, Roberta E. and Uricchio, William, *The Many Lives of the Batman: Critical Approaches to a Superhero and His Media*, Routledge, 1991. Fine symposium of essays on Batman.

Perry, George and Aldridge, Alan, *The Penguin Book of Comics*, Penguin, 1967, New Edition 1989. Hugely influential in the sixties, a new, updated edition is being prepared by Paul Gravett.

Steranko, Jim, *History of Comics*, Supergraphics, 1970 *et. seq.* with a foreword by Federico Fellini . . . 'nuff said.

Comics and Graphic Novels

My personal selection, and guided partly by easy availability, this is only the smallest sampling of the thousands of superhero comics published. It's only by wide reading within the genre that its forms and narrative rules begin to become apparent.

Animal Man 1–26 (DC Comics). The Grant Morrison issues.

Arkham Asylum (DC Comics/Titan Books, 1989). Grant Morrison and Dave McKean. The superhero comic as high art. Pretentious but fun.

The Amazing Spider-Man 1–38 (Marvel Comics). Currently, the first 20 issues are available in hardback reprint. The Lee/Ditko *Spider-Man* that set the tone of Marvel in the 1960s.

Batman: The Dark Knight Returns (DC Comics, 1986). Frank Miller's radical reinterpretation of the Batman myth.

Batman: The Killing Joke (DC Comics/Titan Books, 1988). Alan Moore and Brian Bolland examine the Batman/Joker relationship.

Batman: Year One (DC Comics/Titan Books, 1989). Very good Frank Miller/Dave Mazzuchelli retelling of the Batman origin.

Daredevil – A Lonely Place of Dying (Marvel Comics, 1989). Frank Miller's return to the character that launched his illustrious career.

The Flash 1– (DC Comics). Bill Messner-Loeb and Greg LaRocque: about as good as a contemporary mainstream superhero comic can get.

The Greatest Batman Stories Ever Told (DC Comics/Hamlyn, 1989). A good mix of Batman yarns from 1939 to 1986.

Man of Steel 1–6 (DC Comics). John Byrne's relaunching of the Superman myth after the *Crisis on Infinite Earths*.

Journey Into Mystery/The Mighty Thor 83–179 (Marvel Comics). The early Jack Kirby issues are well worth tracking down.

Miracle Man 1–16 (Eclipse Comics). Alan Moore's British superhero foreshadows many of the later themes and preoccupations of *Watchmen*.

Phantom Lady (Fox Features). Golden Age issues are expensive! Some of Matt Baker's classic artwork for this title has been reprinted in *Good Girl Art Quarterly*.

She-Hulk Graphic Novel (Marvel Comics, 1985). John Byrne's vision of the 6′ 7″ bright green superheroine.

Superman: The Man of Tomorrow (Titan Books, 1988). Conveniently collects together all three Alan Moore Superman stories, but unfortunately only in black and white.

The Uncanny X-Men (Marvel Comics). Issues 108, 109 and 111–143 are the Byrne and Claremont issues. They are highly collectible – i.e. expensive.

Watchmen 1–12 (DC Comics, 1986–87). More conveniently available as a graphic novel, DC Comics/Titan Books, 1988.

NOTES

CHAPTER ONE

1 Superman has been in continuous publication since 1938, Batman since 1939. Wonder Woman has been in continuous publication since 1941, barring a short hiatus in 1986–87.
2 *The Comics Journal*, edited since 1976 by Gary Groth, is the premier fan publication – its intellectual range and acuity of critical discourse is very impressive. *The New Comics* (Berkley Books, 1989), is a collection of interviews with notable artists and writers from the pages of the *Journal*.
3 When does a comic become a graphic novel? 'The most useful distinction in comics is to be drawn between periodical and book-style publication. A periodical is comprised of issues, one of which always replaces the previous one. The title is continuous, but one issue always differs from another. A book is a publication in which the title and issue are the same. A new printing does not require abandoning the contents in favour of a new set. A graphic novel is a unified comic art form that exploits the relationship between the two: book and periodical.' [Steve Edgell, 1992].
4 Batman first appeared in *Detective Comics* 27, 1939; Wonder Woman in *All Star Comics 8*, 1941; the Sub Mariner in *Marvel Comics* 1, 1939. The Arrow first appeared in *Funny Pages* 21 (1938), Shock Gibson in *Speed Comics*, (October 1939) and the Masked Marvel in *Keen Detective Funnies* 11 (1940).
5 Captain America first appeared in *Captain America* 1 (1941). The story is reproduced in Jules Feiffer's *The Great Comic Book Heroes*.
6 The Golden Age lasted from 1938 to 1949. The Silver Age is agreed as having begun in 1956; there is no agreed terminal date, but most would accept that it lasted until around 1967–70.
7 Plastic Man also survived the slump of early fifties, but never cashed in on the new impetus of the Silver Age: publication ceased in 1956.
8 EC's major horror titles were *Vault of Horror*, *Haunt of Fear* and *Crypt of Terror* (later *Tales From the Crypt*), all launched in 1950.
9 Although *Seduction of the Innocent* was published in 1954, Wertham had been campaigning against violence in comic-books since the late forties. In 1948 he presided over a New York Department of Hospitals' symposium called 'The Psychopathology of Comic Books'.
10 The hearings took place as part of the Senate Subcommittee to Investigate Juvenile Delinquency in the United States.
11 Flash reappeared in *Showcase* 4, October 1956. This date is usually regarded as the beginning of the Silver Age.
12 The Green Lantern returned in *Showcase* 22, October 1959.
13 Supergirl premiered in *Action Comics* 252, May 1959.
14 The Justice League of America first appeared *The Brave and the Bold* 28, March 1960. The super-team acquired its own title in October 1960.
15 The Fantastic Four made their debut in *Fantastic Four* 1, November 1961.
16 Spider-Man made his first appearance in *Amazing Fantasy* 15, August 1962 – the very last scheduled issue before this title was axed. *Amazing Spider-Man* 1 followed for March 1963.
17 The X-Men made their debut in *X-Men* 1, September 1963.
18 The Mighty Thor first appeared in *Journey Into Mystery* 83, August 1962. In March 1966 the comic was retitled *The Mighty Thor*, though keeping the numbered sequence from the earlier title.

19 The Incredible Hulk burst on the scene in *The Incredible Hulk* 1, May 1962.
20 Captain America returned to action in *Avengers* 4, May 1964.The Sub Mariner had re-surfaced earlier, in *Fantastic Four* 4, May 1962.
21 The Neal Adams Green Lantern/Green Arrow sequence runs from *Green Lantern* 76 to 89.
22 See, for example 'Drawing The Line' by Buddy Saunders, *Comics Journal* 138, pp. 109–122.
23 Quoted in 'The Man of Tomorrow and the Boys of Yesterday' by Dennis Dooley, from *Superman at Fifty! The Persistence of a Legend!*, ed. Dennis Dooley and Gary Engle, Octavia, 1987, p. 26.
24 *Action Comics* 1 was cover-dated June 1938. This comic is reprinted in *The Smithsonian Book of Comic Book Comics*, ed. Michael Barrier and Martin Williams, Smithsonian Institution Press and Harry N. Abrams, 1981, pp. 19–31. A very similar story appears in *Superman* 1, Summer 1939. This comic is reprinted in *The Great Comic Book* heroes, ed. Jules Feiffer, The Dial Press, 1965, pp. 57–67.
25 *Action Comics* 1, p. 1.
26 *Action Comics* 1, p. 5.
27 *Action Comics* 1, p. 4.
28 *Action Comics* 1, p. 10.
29 See, for example, *The Golden Bough*, by Sir James Frazer, Abridged Edition, Macmillan, 1957, pp. 277–279.
30 The first appearance of the Joker is in *Batman* 1, Spring 1940.
31 This long-running dispute eventually led to the cancellation of *Captain Marvel* and the whole Marvel Family line of comics in 1953. There have been several unsuccessful attempts to revive the original *Captain Marvel* since. Marvel Comics' *Captain Marvel* is a completely different character, who (paradoxically) was much closer in conception to Superman than Fawcett's character ever was.
32 By 1942, there were 143 different comic book titles being published in the United States, with an annual industry revenue of some fifteen million dollars.
33 Several of these characters have appeared in comic-book form. Pulp hero Doc Savage appeared in his own comic in May 1940, when longtime Doc Savage publisher Street and Smith decided to enter the comic-book market. The Green Hornet and Captain Midnight – both heroes of the radio serials – entered the comic medium in 1940 and 1942 respectively.
34 Claude Levi-Strauss, *The View From Afar*, Peregrine, 1987, pp. 259–260.
35 *Fantastic Four* 10, p. 5.
36 Quoted in Bob Kane, *Batman & Me*, Eclipse Books, 1989, p. 44.
37 This was a special Batman edition by Kane and Finger, Summer 1940. The story is reprinted in Kane's *Batman & Me*, pp. 58–70.
38 'New York World's Fair' p. 1.
39 'New York World's Fair' p. 13.
40 'New York World's Fair' p. 13.
41 'New York World's Fair' p. 1.
42 'New York World's Fair' p. 8.
43 Roland Barthes, *Mythologies*, Fontana, 1972, pp. 109–159.

CHAPTER TWO

1 Saussure's terminology is exhaustively defined in the *Course in General Linguistics* (Fontana, 1974). Jonathan Culler's *Saussure* (Fontana, 1976) is a good general introduction to Saussure's thinking.
2 They did so in the excellent 'Midas' saga, *Iron Man* 103–108.
3 *Iron Man* 108, p. 11.
4 See, for example, *Avengers* 170, 194.
5 Ant-Man (Henry Pym) first appeared in *Tales to Astonish* 35, September 1962. He was a founder member of *The Avengers*, September 1963. By

Avengers 7 he turned to growth powers and was renamed Giant Man, an identity he later abandoned to become Yellowjacket, in the classic two-part story *Avengers* 59–60, which contains Pym's marriage to Janet (The Wasp) Van Dyne. In *Avengers* 212 Pym was accused of serious breaches of the Avengers code of conduct, and was court martialed by his fellow Avengers in #212. Pym abandoned the Yellowjacket identity in Avengers 230, though he has since been back in action again.

6 Green Arrow has displayed these characteristics both as a member of the Justice League of America and as a partner to the Green Lantern. See, for example, the contrasting attitudes of Green Arrow and Green Lantern in *Green Lantern/Green Arrow* 78 (July 1970).

7 *Watchmen* 7, p. 28.

8 Moore and Gibbons originally developed the concept of *Watchmen* as a vehicle for characters from the Charlton comics group, for which DC had acquired the rights. Dick Giordano of DC suggested the material was used to develop a totally new set of heroes – partly out of the affection for the old Charlton characters, which he had worked with earlier in his career. See *The New Comics*, ed. Gary Groth and Robert Fiore, Berkley, 1988, p. 97–98.

9 *Watchmen* 7, p. 5.

10 *Watchmen* 7, p. 16.

11 Quoted in the *Great History of Comic Books*, Ron Goulart, Contemporary Books, 1986, p. 142.

12 Fox Features' *Phantom Lady* first appeared in August 1947. Marvel's *Miss Fury* first appearance is dated Winter 1942.

13 Despite the comments from *Ms Magazine* quoted in the *Comics Journal* 144, p. 7. Pamela Robin Brandt praises the personality and powers of the She-Hulk and other superheroines.

14 There are other comics that have featured a top superhero regularly teamed with a less-known character. *Marvel Team-Up* featured Spider-Man plus one, *Marvel Two-In-One* The Thing plus friends. Superman team-ups have been featured in DC's *The World's Finest Comics.*

15 *Crisis On Infinite Earths* 1, April 1985 was a first step towards re-ordering the entire DC universe. Another key element was the re-telling of the Superman myth from scratch in *The Man of Steel* mini series (#1 June 1986)

16 *Superman* 423 (September 1986), p. 1.

17 T.S. Eliot, *Selected Essays*, Faber, 1932, p. 15.

18 In *Avengers* 4, March 1964.

19 Captain America should by the early nineties be well over fifty years old, even allowing for those years in the ice.

20 See, for example, *Fantastic Four* 1, November 1961, p. 16. Susan Storm admonishes Ben Grimm to agree to pilot her brother's untested experimental rocket: 'Ben, we've got to take that chance . . . unless we want the Commies to beat us to it! I – I never thought that YOU would be a coward!.'

21 'Out of the many, the one.'

22 Edmund Leach, *Levi-Strauss*, Fontana, 1970, p. 116.

23 *Fantastic Four* 87, June 1969, p. 22.

24 Catherine Yronwode, for example: one-time number one correspondent to superhero letter columns, now proprietor of Eclipse Comics.

25 Although Morrison's *Animal Man* has played every possible trick and post-modernist self-reflexive game with the process of continuity. See issues 1–26.

26 The Kree are alien race from which Marvel Comics 1960s' version of Captain Marvel sprung. Bizarro is a strange, backwards version of Superman, who lives on a cube-shaped planet and is Superman's 'imperfect-perfect' duplicate.

27 See *Detective Comic* 31, p. 5. The story is reprinted in *The Greatest Batman Stories Ever Told*, ed. Dick Giordano, Hamlyn, 1989, p. 18.

28 See *Detective Comics* 168, p. 13. The story is reprinted in *The Greatest Joker Stories Ever Told* ed. Mike Gold, DC, 1988, p. 63.

29 Roland Barthes, *Mythologies*, Fontana, 1972, p. 25.
30 See *Action Comics* 583, p. 23.

CHAPTER THREE

1 From *Captain Marvel* 100, 1949. The text of this comic is reprinted in *A Smithsonian Book of Comic Book Comics*, pp. 81–113.
2 *Action Comics* 1, p. 1. Reprinted in *A Smithsonian Book of Comic Book Comics*, pp. 19–31.
3 For another view of this, see 'A Loaf of Bread, A Jug of Wine and Eddie Campbell', an interview with Sam Yang, *The Comics Journal* 145, p. 81.
4 *Thor* 282 – 300 were developed from the *Niebelungenlied*, and included a version of Thor incarnated as Siegfried.
5 See the *New Larrousee Dictionary of Mythology*, Hamlyn, 1968, p. 252.
6 See, for example, *Avengers* 174, where Thor is defeated in a battle with the villainous Collector, and has to be revived by the other Avengers afterwards with a bucket of cold water.
7 *Avengers* 149, p. 31.
8 See Joseph Campbell, *The Hero With A Thousand Faces*, Princeton University Press, 2nd Edition 1968, p. 148.
9 See Sigmund Freud, *On Sexuality*, Pelican, 1977, p. 221.
10 *See Superman at Fifty*!, ed Dennis Dooley and Gary Engle, Octavia Press, 1987. In particular, the article 'What Makes Superman So Darned American?' by Gary Engle, op. cit. pp. 79–87.
11 'For the man Who Has Everything' is from *Superman Annual* 11, 1984. 'Whatever happened to the man of Tomorrow' is from *Superman* 423 and *Action Comics* 583, 1986.
12 *Superman Annual* 11, p. 8.
13 *Superman* 11, 1987, p. 14.
14 See 'The Good, the Bad and the Oedipal' by Lester Roebuck, from *Superman at Fifty*!, p. 151.
15 See Sir James Frazer, *The Golden Bough*, Abridged Edition Macmillan 1957, p. 183.
16 See *Batman* 47, 1948, and *Detective Comics* 235, 1956. Both these stories have been reprinted more than once: both are included in *The Greatest Batman Stories Ever Told*, Hamlyn, 1989.
17 A recent example is the opening panels of the Archie Goodwin/Dan Jurgens/ Dick Giordano *Detective Comics Annual* 1990, which open with Batman standing beside his parents' moonlit grave.
18 This theme is explored in several Batman texts, such as the Alan Moore/Brian Bolland *The Killing Joke* (1988) and the Grant Morrison/Dave McKean *Arkham Asylum* (1989).
19 *Detective Comics* 500, 1981, pp. 5–6. The story is also included in *The Greatest Batman Stories Ever Told.*
20 *Detective Comics* 500, pp. 9–10.
21 *Detective Comics* 500, p. 18.
22 *Detective Comics* 500, p. 19.
23 *Detective Comics* 500, p. 2 and p. 17.
24 *Detective Comics* 500, p. 2 and p. 17.
25 *Captain America* 177, p. 10.
26 *Avengers* 194, p. 3.
27 Magneto's first appearance was in *X-Men* 1, 1963. The Brotherhood of Evil Mutants first appeared in *X-Men* 4. Two members of the original Brotherhood of Evil Mutants – the Scarlet Witch and her brother Quicksilver – later reformed and joined the Avengers.
28 See, also, letters in *X-Men* 116, 117, 149 and 154 for broad interpretations of the series' overall meaning.
29 See, for example, the argument in *Avengers* 175, pp. 22–23.

30 See, for example, the *She-Hulk Graphic Novel*, Marvel, 1985, p. 10–11. 'I'm six foot seven and green! People are gonna stare no matter how I dress!' says the She-Hulk, in answer to her boyfriend's suggestion that her white PVC outfit is a little too revealing for streetwear.
31 Umberto Eco, *Travels in Hyper Reality*, Picador, 1986, p. 74.
32 An interesting sidelight on the comics/Cold War debate is shed by the article on Charles Atlas 'The Insult That made a Man Out of Mac' by Mark Brett, the *Comics Journal* 144, pp. 87–90. Brett argues a convincing case for Charles Atlas and his Dynamic Tension bodybuilding courses as cultural metaphors for the Cold War.
33 See Jean Baudrillard, *America*, Verso, 1988. Of particular interest is the chapter 'Utopia achieved', pp. 75–105.

CHAPTER FOUR

1 Jack Kirby's early-sixties artwork for *The Fantastic Four* and *Thor* is one of the touchstones of superhero art. Steve Ditko, by comparison, is an oddball whose style seemed to be exactly right for *Spider-Man*, but often out of key with the feel of other titles and characters. His early *Doctor Strange* material, though currently in vogue, seems less successful with the passage of time.
2 Sheldon Moldoff had worked on the *Green Lantern* as early as 1940. Wayne Boriney worked on *Superman* titles in the fifties.
3 Magneto subsequently became leader of the X-Men, after his trial in *X-Men* 200. But he has since returned to his hostility to homo sapiens.
4 Claremont took over the scripting in *X-Men* 94.
5 Byrne's artwork first appeared in *X-Men* 108.
6 See *X-Men* 116, p. 2–3, *X-Men* 115, p. 2–3 and *X-Men* 122, p. 7.
7 *X-Men* 122, p. 3.
8 See the interview with Byrne in the *Comics Journal* 51.
9 Theodore Sturgeon, *More Than Human* (1953), reissue Gollancz, 1986.
10 *X-Men* 108, p. 30.
11 *X-Men* 123, p. 17.
12 Arcade is yet another Oedipal figure. In *X-Men* 124, p. 2, he explains that 'on my twenty-first birthday, my father cut off my allowance. The next day I cut of my daddy's life.'
13 *X-Men* 124, p. 26.
14 In the 1985 *X-Men* 'Heroes For Hope' special issue, the short section scripted by Claremont shows Storm being offered a series of personae: Earth Mother, All-American Girl, Happy Home-Maker, Free Spirit, Wanton. 'Pieces of myself, these may well be . . . but not the whole!' she comments.
15 It all happens in *X-Men* 129–137.
16 Collectors regularly pay much more for old comics, but the superhero graphic novel is considerably more expensive when new than the traditional 6×9 in four-colour comic. Such additional expense reflects its potential 'adult' market.
17 See, for example, the images on pages (a)8,9,24–25, (b)5, and 9–10.
18 *The Dark Knight Returns*, p. (a) 16.
19 *The Dark Knight Returns*, p. (a) 37.
20 See Watchmen 10, p. 8.
21 *The Dark Knight Returns*, p. (a) 39.
22 *The Dark Knight Returns*, p. (b) 9–10.
23 See *Captain America* 177–184.
24 In the Ron Mann documentary *Comic Book Confidential*, first shown on Channel 4 in 1990.
25 *The Dark Knight Returns*, p. (c) 21.
26 *The Dark Knight Returns*, p. (c) 41.
27 *The Dark Knight Returns*, p. (b) 15–16.
28 *The Dark Knight Returns*, p. (a) 47.
29 *Watchmen* 2, p. 13.

30 *Watchmen* 2, p. 18.
31 This point is very forcefully made in *Watchmen* 5, p. 28, when Rorschach is arrested and his mask is pulled off. 'No! My face! Give it back!' he shouts. 'This ugly little zero is the terror of the underworld' says one of the police. Rorschach is nothing without his mask.
32 *Watchmen* 2, p. 30.
33 *Watchmen* 10, p. 32.
34 *Watchmen* 11, p. 31.
35 *Watchmen* 5, pp. 29–32 contains extracts from a bogus history of comics, the *Treasure Island Treasury of Comics*, 'Flint Editions, New York, 1984'.
36 *Watchmen* 5, p. 31.
37 *Watchmen* 3, p. 1.
38 *Watchmen* 3, p. 1.
39 *Watchmen* 3, p. 2.
40 *Watchmen* 3, p. 2.
41 *Watchmen* 3, p. 2.
42 *Watchmen* 2, p. 10.
43 *Watchmen* 2, p. 10.
44 *Watchmen* 2, p. 10.
45 From 'Big Words' (Alan Moore interview), *The Comics Journal* 138, p. 75.
46 *The Comics Journal* 138, p. 73.

INDEX

Figures in *italics* refer to illustrations